Praying the Sacred in Secular Settings

D1522549

Praying the Sacred in Secular Settings

Gail E. Bowman

Chalice Press®

St. Louis, Missouri

2000

All scripture quotations, unless otherwise indicated, are from the *New Revised Standard Version Bible*, copyright 1989, Division of Christian Education of the National Council of the Churches of Christ in the USA. Used by permission. All rights reserved.

Cover design: Mike Foley
Interior design: Elizabeth Wright
Art direction: Elizabeth Wright

This book is printed on acid-free, recycled paper.

Visit Chalice Press on the World Wide Web at
www.chalicepress.com

10 9 8 7 6 5 4 3 2 1   00 01 02 03

Library of Congress Cataloging–in–Publication Data

Bowman, Gail E.
  Praying the sacred in secular settings / by Gail E. Bowman.
      p.   cm.
  ISBN 0-8272-2962-3
  1. Prayer–Christianity.   2. Public worship.   I. Title.
  BV226.B69 2000
  264'.1 — dc21   00–008622
                                                          CIP

Printed in the United States of America

To Johnnetta Cole, and Glenda Price,
educators, around whom and because of whom
great growth takes place

And to my sister, Linda Susan Bowman Lane,
the good deacon,
who gives my ministry wings
and smiles

Contents

Introduction

Four years of seminary did nothing to alter my opinion that ministry is a threshold to be crossed only when all other options have been checked, exhausted, and checked again. Initially, I did not believe I had the background for any kind of sacred work, nor the temperament, ability, or, in some ways, the inclination. Nevertheless, I had received a very startling and former-days-shattering "call," had left a legal career without much regret, and was experiencing a deeply consuming curiosity coupled with hope that continued to urge me forward. After four years of study, a parish position as a youth minister, and an administrative position at a seminary, I was still at the "Who, me?" stage, amazed to be doing what I was doing.

As has been the case for so many other people, the Divine persuaded me into a situation that would demand broad and deep growth by offering me the apparently delectable carrot of something I was sure I wanted. Eyes pinned on the bright excitement of preaching regularly to young women who would not find my rather odd and truly unorthodox style and approach unnerving, I came to Spelman College in Atlanta, Georgia, in February 1993. I was to be the new college minister; the former college minister was stepping down after forty-one years in the position.

A historically black liberal arts college for women with a student population of around nineteen hundred, Spelman is well known, especially in the black community, for the high quality of its students, education, and overall experience. It was not my first time working with young people, nor was it my first time working in a historically black institution of higher learning, but I had a lot to learn about working in this new setting.

Although modest in endowment and acreage, Spelman is fabulously wealthy in history, tradition, blessing, and talent. The students have a very clear sense of themselves. So, while still learning what it meant to be a minister, and just then learning what it meant to be a *college* minister, I was about to be enrolled in a crash course of American-South/Georgia-Black/female-late 1990s-Spelmanite spirituality and religion.

Fumbling my way forward, I quizzed the former college minister about his experiences and understanding, haunted the city library reading books on everything from sacred worship spaces to Sherman's march to the sea, and spent several afternoons sitting on the floor of the publications office poring over back issues of the college magazine. All the while, my priority continued to be sermon preparation, because I was convinced that preaching was the main task that God had brought me to Spelman to perform.

It is not an exaggeration to say that less than five percent of Spelman College's population—students, faculty, and staff included—ever heard me preach a sermon. During my first semester, on one landmark Sunday morning in historic Sisters Chapel with its capacity of one thousand, fully eleven young women put in an appearance for worship. I prayed a silent prayer that day that if God would always give me at least eleven on Sunday morning (keeping in mind how well Jesus worked with twelve), I would do everything in my mental, physical, and spiritual capability to hold up my end of the ministry with grace and humility.

It was at that point that I began noticing that while hardly anyone ever heard me preach, almost everyone heard me pray—but most of these occasions would not be worship. The college used prayer at convocations, dedications, town hall meetings, and almost all occurrences of communal joy, sorrow, and food consumption. The task of public, non-worship prayer was one I undertook with great care.

Although Spelman was founded as a Christian institution (the motto: Our Whole School for Christ), by the late twentieth century almost every religion of the world was represented among its student body and, particularly, the faculty. This was my first challenge—learning to share public prayer in ways that were truly inclusive of the community. Potent a dilemma as could be, the second challenge was greater: how to pray in the moment and the setting, with a range of ages, races, tastes, and circumstances represented, something that was worthy of the children of God.

Over time and through tremendous blessing, ministry has won my heart. My work affords me innumerable opportunities to use almost everything I have and everything I am, and that is great joy. My work has also planted in me an intense and steadily growing love for the children of God and a sense of involvement—in the world, with people, in the divine and continuing creative act. This sense is a wholly unexpected wonder.

In the midst of ministry's benefits I have been able to make my peace with the reality of the sacred moment of expectation, those moments through which we enter into communal prayer. I now perceive that my moments of intimidation are truly God's moments of anticipation. I could not repeatedly stand before "the public" and proclaim a group or a project that is purely secular in nature. But I can and do stand before almost anyone, and almost any group, and proclaim God. In those moments and in the preparation for those moments, I am honored beyond expression and beyond measure.

1

The Idea of Public Prayer

Gently, gently do You lead them;
Gently, gently, show me how.

There is something special about public prayer. The nature and composition of the group being prayed for and with will vary, but the essential nature of public prayer does—must—remain the same. Public prayer involves a kind of interior and communal travel. In it, the leader calls upon Power that is unseen and only partly understood to carry the group, as a group, into a realm of awe and surety from which they will emerge changed. To accomplish this, the leader needs to lead while being led, and to be convicted of the need for and value of not just prayer, but *public* prayer.

Prayer speaks to the deep realities of the nature of being human. It is about what we are and what we are not. It is a spiritual communion that, in its fullest intensity, is also physical and psychological. Both the yearning for prayer and the struggle against it are serious and significant.

Public prayer is more. Public prayer celebrates the sacredness of people gathered together purposefully and for good. It is a leap of faith, a risk, that is tremendous and (of course) *very* public. Public prayer is a call, a response, a stretching forth of the open hand of the soul; it is opportunity. To be asked to offer public prayer—invocations, benedictions, and other formal and informal offerings—is both awe(ful) and glorious.

The requirement that one stand regularly before a group of people, everyone silent, all eyes turned to you, would prompt a degree of reverence in just about anyone. For some people, functioning in such moments would be agony. For some it would even be impossibility. Because of sermons and public prayers, ministers and others who assume leadership roles in the church ply their trade in those moments of expectant, sometimes needy silence. It is not an appropriate neighborhood for the timid.

Public prayer in the context of single-faith worship is a concept about which some few (and certainly not many) books have been written. But public prayer for multi-faith communities in contexts other than worship is a very particular undertaking about which precious little has been written. Pastors and laypersons offer multi-faith, non-worship prayer occasionally. College ministers, chaplains, and deans of chapel offer such prayers often. Indeed, working beyond the setting of worship, such clergy are frequently offering prayer for persons who are members of their community but not members of their congregation. Faced with this reality, I quickly determined that it was necessary to develop a style and an approach to such prayers that had the benefit of integrity and the potential for quality. A better understanding of both of my background traditions—African American and Christian—has not answered all my questions, but has proven helpful.

The black church tradition in the United States is famous for a prayer style that is eloquent, rhythmic, practical, and humble. Its roots reach back through the generations, perhaps all the way to the ancestors. Such prayers are not written; they are delivered spontaneously, extemporaneously, with great group participation and support.

A spontaneous offering of prayers is understood to be evidence that God initiates and carries the prayer forth…Prayers printed in the bulletin to be prayed (or read) together by the congregation have little appeal to many Black worshipers. This limits the possibility of spontaneity and for some lacks the natural approach to God under the power of the Spirit. Operative here is the understanding that one called upon to pray must yield to the power of God, who speaks with the folks directly when they close their eyes, open their mouths, and rely on the enabling power of the Spirit to fill them. To read or pray words that are written, no matter how carefully they reflect another's spiritual direction, is to interfere with the natural form of communication between the divine and humanity…One of the most difficult assignments for theological students is to prepare various forms of prayers in writing.[1]

When the traditional African American style is invoked, black Christians—National Baptist Churches to the Church of God in Christ—are all bathed in the warm comfort of familiarity. These prayers have their own beauty, but because they draw on a shared history, oral tradition, and group dynamic, they are most appropriate in the context of worship, particularly in predominantly black worship.

Because the traditional African American worship-style prayers are extemporaneous, they have not been recorded until recently, as churches have begun audio- and videotaping worship services. Even now, these prayers are recorded but not examined or studied. Not surprisingly then, very little has been written *about* African American extemporaneous prayers, although there are a few historical collections of prayers that were written, either before delivery or after. James Weldon

---

[1] Melva Wilson Costen, *African American Christian Worship* (Nashville: Abingdon Press, 1993), 106–7.

Johnson's sermon series *God's Trombones*[2] includes the prayer
with perhaps the most famous line of the African American
tradition—we come as "empty pitchers to a full fountain"[3]—
but it would not be accurate to say that African American
extemporaneous prayer is always characterized by such compelling choices of language. Its main strengths are fervor, simplicity, sincerity, humility, and "common ground" phrases that
stir the praying spirits of those who are part of the tradition.
Aside from firm cautions against the writing out of prayers,
there is not much material written from the African American
perspective about the composition and delivery of public
prayers.

In addition to having the *Book of Common Prayer* to its
credit, the white church tradition has spawned books that address the issue of structuring and delivering prayers candidly.
Two of the better volumes are *Leading in Public Prayer* by Andrew W. Blackwood and *Effective Public Prayer* by Robert
Williamson. Both Blackwood and Williamson make cautious
allowance for "extempore" or "free" prayer but firmly oppose
"unpremeditated" or "unprepared" prayer. Blackwood quotes
Nathaniel Micklem writing about "extempore prayer":

> Ex tempore prayer is not to be identified with unpre-
> meditated prayer. I have never understood why the
> holy Spirit should require a minister to prepare the
> words of his sermon in his study and should disap-
> prove of the preparation of his prayers.[4]

According to Blackwood, a free prayer is not prepared in form
but *is* prepared in substance.

Williamson quotes preacher J. H. Jowett as he expresses his
concern about "unprepared" prayer:

---

[2] *God's Trombones* is still presented in its entirety by individuals and speaker groups coupled
with musicians. Traditionally, it is presented from memory; no notes, texts, or manuscripts are
used.

[3] James Weldon Johnson, *God's Trombones: Seven Negro Sermons in Verse* (New York: Pen-
guin Books, 1990), 13.

[4] Andrew W. Blackwood, *Leading in Public Prayer* (Nashville: Abingdon Press, 1958), 24–
25.

The real danger of an unprepared prayer is that it may fail to lead anywhere. It may merely skip about on the surface, becoming, as Jowett has said, "a disorderly dance of empty words, going we know not whither—a mob of words carrying no blood, bearing no secret of the soul..." Instead of the people's being drawn near to the heart of God, they may only be shuffled about from one thought to another...and at the end of the prayer be no better off than they were before.[5]

The concerns of the two traditions, taken together, constitute a two-part wisdom. Leaders who use written prayers might be cautioned against the hazard of reading their prayers instead of praying them, bringing inadequate fervor to the endeavor, and resisting the movement of the Holy Spirit, who might, in the midst of prayer, want to make some additions or deletions.

Leaders who use extemporaneous prayers might be cautioned against a changeless week-to-week pattern of prayers that fails to take into consideration the particularities of occasion and persons present (or absent) and fails to address the joys and concerns of the world outside the congregation. The hazard of extemporaneous prayers is that the traditional can sometimes become too comfortable, allowing listener-participants to be carried along on a wave of familiarity, hearing little and altering nothing, locked in a time warp of isolation from the ever-changing world.

It is possible for a public prayer style to celebrate the best of both traditions. I pursue this intriguing intersection because of my strong affection and respect for both praying styles. I appreciate the traditional African American approach with its sincerity, simplicity, and humility, and its rhythms, alliteration, and love of language. It makes allowance for my love of poetry and prose, music lyrics, imagery, and imagination. I also have a

---

[5]Robert L. Williamson, *Effective Public Prayer* (Nashville: Broadman Press, 1960), 9. See J. H. Jowett, *The Preacher, His Life and Work* (Garden City, N.Y.: Doubleday, 1928), 152.

great deal of respect for the white traditional style that favors detailed preparation of prayers in advance and provides some guidance for that process, as well as for the delivery of prayers. Both traditions continue to teach me.

Preparing public prayers provides some of the most re-markable experiences of my ministry. I am, by now, calmly ritualistic about it. I prepare myself carefully, listen intently, struggle at great length for just the right words, and then ready myself with a firm hand. All of this takes time. I worked, off and on, for two days once, preparing a prayer for the UNICEF Child Survival Awards dinner in Atlanta. Countless hours were invested, but the result was what I had prayed for—that prayer is one of the ones, in my belief, that said almost precisely what the Spirit asked to have said.

Like preaching, prayer is mostly a gift of the Spirit but is also immensely hard work, shamelessly demanding of the totality of the pray-er's being. Whatever you have—talent, experience, wisdom, intelligence, innocence, dogged determination, love and longing, joy and pain, a strong sense of justice, courage—is demanded of you in the preparation for and delivery of public prayer. Public prayer is serious. It is real. It is special.

2

Appreciating Prayer

"It's me, it's me, it's me, O Lord,
Standin' in the need of prayer.
Not my brother, not my sister,
but it's me, O Lord,
Standin' in the need of prayer."[1]

For me, prayers begin with a sense of some kind—that they need to include a hymn, or that there is a particular feeling to be invoked, or that there will be a visual or auditory element present at the moment of prayer that is not to be denied. Prayers are more willing to be written and delivered when that essential element is sought after and honored. The simple way to perceive this would probably be to say that I am searching for the prayer's purpose.[2] Much happier in the world of imagery, however, I call that sense, that focal point or animating element, "the door."

---

[1]"Standin' in the Need of Prayer," traditional African American spiritual.
[2]Andrew W. Blackwood, *Leading in Public Prayer* (Nashville: Abingdon Press, 1958), 157.

11

Tactile as I am, prayer preparation (and sermon preparation) always gives me the sensation of a precious orb, a hollow sphere of indeterminate (but not small) size. I am positioned outside the sphere. I know that the sphere is the prayer in its original and God-intended form. The sphere waits to combine its celestial energies with my terrestrial sensitivities, proclivities, and "sack material."[3] It favors this conjoining. But to accomplish it, I must work from the inside, I must find the way in, I must find or be shown the door. I can identify aspects and elements of the prayer without finding the door, but its concept is not fully conceived, and I cannot begin to prepare in earnest, until I do.

I must admit I expected to learn more about the composition of public prayers in seminary than I did. I learned little about composition, but I learned a great deal about the necessity for and the power of prayer; this was certainly the "better part."

Almost all my seminary class sessions began with prayer. I was a part-time evening student for my first two years and sped across town to class after a full day's work. Prayer was just what I needed to set the day aside and ready myself for the evening's efforts. Later, when I was in field education that required me to commute from Washington, D.C., to Reston, Virginia, on Sunday mornings at eight and not return until midnight, the Monday prayers were precisely what was required to gather the scattered pieces of myself back together and move on.

I remember one Monday evening prayer done by my church history professor and field education supervisor, Calvin Morris. We were in prayer so long and so earnestly that when we opened our eyes, our pupils needed time to readjust to the classroom lights. Yet, in that time, Calvin had identified if not all, then most of the joys and sorrows, frustrations and satisfactions of ministry in its disparate forms and lifted them up to

---

[3]For more about sack material, see chapter 3.

God. I felt cleansed; I *was* cleansed. It was only later that I recognized and appreciated the work Calvin had done for all of us with that prayer. Calvin also frequently used hymn lines in prayer and as prayer. I attribute my affection for this style to him.

Prayers of the people or "pastoral prayers," the longest and most detailed of the "official" prayers of Christian worship, include four or five elements that constitute an acrostic: adoration, confession of sin, thanksgiving, supplication (petitions and intercessions), and (sometimes included as a part of the prayer and sometimes not) submission or service.[4] The acrostic is ACTS or ACTSS.

- In adoration—God's holiness is proclaimed.

- In confession—the congregation's failure to live in ways that are consistent with the Christian commitment is recognized.

- In thanksgiving—God's forgiveness of sin is celebrated. This is also called the declaration of pardon.

- In supplication—the needs and desires of those present are voiced as petitions, and concerns for persons and circumstances beyond the congregation are expressed as intercessions.[5]

It is unusual to encounter pastoral prayers outside the context of worship services or other religious gatherings. Instead, invocations and benedictions are the two prayer styles that appear on the programs of secular events with the most frequency.

Although some assume that the purpose of an invocation is to "call up" the Spirit of God or "cause" the Spirit of God to be present in a place or at an event, people of faith cringe at this theology and proclaim it unsound. Because we believe

---

[4]Blackwood, *Leading in Public Prayer,* 27.
[5]Ibid., 41–58.

that God is present everywhere and always, there is certainly no need to call God into places or circumstances that are already God's to begin with.

Traditional native African religions are structured in a way that celebrates the omnipresence of the sacred and the absence of the secular:

> Because traditional religions permeate all the departments of life, there is no formal distinction between the sacred and the secular, between the religious and the non-religious, between the spiritual and the material areas of life. Wherever the African is, there is his religion: he carries it to the fields where he is sowing seeds or harvesting a new crop; he takes it with him to the beer party or to attend a funeral ceremony…Although many African languages do not have a word for religion as such, it nevertheless accompanies the individual from long before his birth to long after his physical death.[6]

This is probably one of the reasons why African Americans seem to be reasonably comfortable with worship and prayer in so-called secular spaces. From worship in the grape arbors and woods to worship in storefront churches and living rooms, African Americans will seek God's blessing almost anywhere.

In addition, Christian theology acknowledges that we cannot "order" God to do anything; God is omnipotent and God is free.[7] God is responsive to us out of mercy and love, but does not take instructions from us. Indeed, the purpose of prayer is not to ask God to move to be near to us, but to adjust our thinking and perceiving to bring us near to God.

---

[6]John S. Mbiti, *African Religions and Philosophy* (Garden City, N.Y.: Doubleday, 1969), 2–3.

[7]"[God's] sovereignty requires that [God] be absolutely free, which means [God] must be free to do whatever [God] wills to do anywhere at any time to carry out [the Divine] eternal purpose in every single detail without interference. Were [God] less than free [God] would be less than sovereign…God is said to be absolutely free because no one and no thing can hinder [God] or compel [God] or stop [God]." A.W. Tozer, *The Knowledge of the Holy: The Attributes of God, Their Meaning in the Christian Life* (New York: Harper, 1961), 170.

An invocation is an opportunity for the group gathered to acknowledge and honor the presence of God. In addition, it is the moment for a commitment to be made that the event about to take place will be conducted in such a way that God will be able to look with favor on the efforts of the persons present and encourage an appropriately grateful, God-acknowledging, and God-praising attitude in them.

An invocation is the most commonly requested public prayer for secular events. In such situations, several challenges may be anticipated. First, the event is likely to be held in something other than sacred space. Despite a perception of God's presence everywhere, and there being no truly "secular" space, rising to offer prayer in a hotel ballroom or school auditorium can be a bit distressing to the spirit of the pray-er, at least initially. This is especially true when the pray-er has the sense that the purpose of the invocation is to "get the God business out of the way" so that the event can move on to more enjoyable and "real" business.

The dilemma is not just the nature of the space, it is also the nature of those who are gathered. In church or chapel it is safe to assume that most of those who are gathered want to be there and believe that they are engaged in an exercise with some inherent value. At retirement parties, building dedications, and junior commencements, a "mixed bag" of people who participate in prayer, people who tolerate prayer, and people who resent prayer are scattered across the room in unpredictable pockets, all caught in a sacred moment of expectation that may or may not hold meaning for them.

Under those circumstances the task is twofold. First, there is work to be done—the people need to be blessed (whether they want to be or not), any food to be consumed or already being consumed needs to be blessed, and God needs to be exalted and thanked. Second, there may—*may*—be an opportunity to do a bit more than the obvious. Depending on the tone of the event, and indeed on the tone of the introduction of the invocation, there may be a chance to make a brief and surprise visit into the sphere of the awe-inspiring. The first part of the task can be done in perfunctory fashion, if the pray-er so chooses. The second part of the task will require courage.

Benedictions, which date back to Jewish synagogue worship, are not technically prayers. The benediction is the concluding opportunity for the mercy of God to be shared with the people and received by them through faith.[8] In sacred settings, congregations do not and probably should not depart without having received the benediction. Rev. Dr. Kenneth Lee Samuels of Victory Baptist Church in Stone Mountain, Georgia, likens the benediction to a cap, the completing piece of worship, without which the worship service in its totality cannot be fully retained. He paints the picture of the problems that would follow purchasing a soft drink in an open cup from a store and leaving without receiving the cap to cover it and prevent it from spilling. Blackwood might agree, claiming that worship is not complete without the benediction:

> If [the benediction] were missing, or spoken as though inconsequential, the people might feel a sense of loss. In some congregations abroad, if the minister inadvertently fails to perform this accustomed rite, the people remain in their pews until he returns and completes what he has begun and carried through almost to the end.[9]

Most churchgoers recognize benedictory language when they hear it and are aware that much of it is scriptural:

> The Lord bless thee and keep thee; the Lord make his face shine upon thee, and be gracious unto thee: The Lord lift up his countenance upon thee, and give thee peace. (Num. 6:24–26, KJV)

---

[8]Blackwood, *Leading in Public Prayer,* 78–79.
[9]Ibid., 77.

Grace, mercy and peace, from God our Father and Jesus Christ our Lord. (1 Tim. 1:2, KJV)

The grace of our Lord Jesus Christ be with you all. Amen. (Phil. 4:23, KJV)

Even the language, "And let all the people say Amen," commonly used as a means of inviting listener–pray-ers to share in the closing of prayer, is taken from scripture (Ps. 106:48).

Blackwood identifies twenty-four scripture passages that are used for benedictions.[10] *The Star Book for Ministers*[11] includes several of the most commonly used passages in its chapter on benedictions. Although scripture forms the foundation for most Christian benedictions, modern benedictions often also include additional language, some of it written by the pastor, that becomes a touchstone for that particular person or congregation. It is also not unusual to experience benedictions that have been specially prepared to accompany and reiterate the main point of the sermon or the occasion.

Not everyone is accustomed to benedictions, but almost everyone is accustomed to "caps." Anyone who is practiced at listening to television or radio news is accustomed to a ritualistic closing word. News programs are not considered over until the "good-night" or "and this is our world" or "and that's the way it is" has been spoken. Even some public events have their traditional words of dismissal: "Good night, travel home safely, see you next year!" Congregations aren't the only groups who wait stubbornly for their event to be "capped" in an appropriate fashion. Who hasn't had the experience of a wonderful event that fell flat at the very end because the words of dismissal were no more than a mumbled, "Oh. A-h-h. Thanks for coming," or even worse, "I guess that's everything. Go home."

---

[10]Genesis 31:49; Numbers 6:24–26; Romans 1:7 and 15:13; 1 Corinthians 1:3; 2 Corinthians 3:17 and 13:13; Galatians 1:3–5 and 6:18; Ephesians 1:2 and 6:23–24; Philippians 4:7 and 4:23; 1 Thessalonians 1:1; 2 Thessalonians 2:16–17, 3:5, and 3:16; 1 Timothy 1:2; Titus 1:4; Hebrews 13:20–21; 1 Peter 5:10; 2 Peter 1:2; 2 John 3; and Revelation 1:4–5.

[11]Edward T. Hiscox, *The Star Book for Ministers* (Valley Forge, Pa.: Judson Press, 1968).

For this reason, benedictions are typically received with tolerance unless the event has been so long and tedious that the attendees are about to shriek with the need to be in motion away from the place. Churchgoers and Sunday stay-at-home-ers alike attend to the act of receiving benediction with patience—they know that in no time at all they will be on their way.

Benedictions are more proclamations or pronouncements than they are prayer. They are not addressed to God; they are addressed to the people of God.[12] Two things immediately indicate a benediction. First, there is the requisite posture: head up (rather than bowed), eyes on the people, hand or hands lifted. Second, there is the phrase "And now..." or "And now may...," which, although optional, signals "benediction" loud and clear. In offering the benediction, the pray-er gets to enjoy something almost all people enjoy: having the last word. Even better, because of the benediction, the last word is God's.

---

[12]Blackwood, *Leading in Public Prayer,* 78.

3

The Technique behind the Task

"Pray because everything depends on God,
and work as though everything depends on you."[1]

I believe that the words of prayer—particularly public, inter-faith, secular setting prayer—must be selected with the utmost care. In such prayers there is a need to be inclusive that is coupled with the need for the prayer leader to be true to her or his own faith. Public prayers must be corporate: "The [prayer]...is leading the people as they pray...It is not his [or her] voice that speaks but the voice of the church [group]."[2] And *all* prayers need to honor the setting, the group, and the occasion.

Beautiful prayers that are also meaningful has been one of my goals. My conviction is that prayer should courageously plumb the depths of both the moment and those things that are eternal and relate to the moment. In addition, the prayer should be worth listening to, compelling, urging the listener

---

[1] Andrew W. Blackwood, *Leading in Public Prayer* (Nashville: Abingdon Press, 1958), 8.
[2] Robert L. Williamson, *Effective Public Prayer* (Nashville: Broadman Press, 1960), 18–19.

to become listener-participant."As a whole, and in every part, a public prayer ought to be interesting. Interesting to whom? To the people whom the prayer leader wishes to lead Godward."[3]

Apparently, it is not only women who appreciate beautiful prayers:

> Every prayer ought to have a quiet beauty. Otherwise, how could it make people think rightly toward God, the Creator of all beauty? On a special occasion the prayers may well have the sort of splendor that belongs to Him.[4]

Beauty in prayers is as much outgrowth as it is intent. "If a leader's heart is moved, and if he [or she] lets his [or her] heart have its way Godward, simple beauty will come."[5]

Meaningful prayer is occasion-, setting-, leader-, and listener-appropriate. It is also theologically sound. Meaningful prayer is a true expression of both what we are and what we aspire to be; it is the claim and the declaration that lifts us a little higher and pulls us a little closer—closer together and closer to God.

Williamson recommends prayer language that is dignified, varied, clear, stimulating, and reverent.[6] He adds that the thought and the language should be fresh.[7] When the choice is between a short word and a long one, Blackwood favors choosing the short word and adds:

> People are more interested in a prayer about persons than in one about abstractions; in one full of facts than one that abounds in theories; and in one with motion like that of a brook on its way toward the sea, more

---

[3]Blackwood, *Leading in Public Prayer*, 161.
[4]Williamson, *Effective Public Prayer*, 163.
[5]Blackwood, *Leading in Public Prayer*, 163.
[6]Williamson, *Effective Public Prayer*, 65–78.
[7]Ibid., 23.

than in lack of onward movement, as in a pond with no outlet.[8]

As I perceive it, because Hebrews 4:16 encourages us to *come boldly unto the throne of grace,* prayer language should be bold. Because so many of my listener-participants are young people and today's young people are part of a highly visual generation, I believe prayer language should paint mental pictures. Perhaps this is what Williamson meant when he urged us to use "word[s] that appeal to the 'eye of the soul.'"[9] There is no need to appeal to the "eye" of the soul alone, however. I endeavor to use language that engages the other senses also.

The most important thing about words, however, is that we must remember that words are worker bees and not the queen of the hive. The purpose of the prayer—its focal point, its animating element, its *door*—is paramount, and everything else finds its sole usefulness in the degree to which it serves that end. No matter how carefully selected, thesaurus-mined, or alliteration-lit the words, if they fail to move the prayer in the direction it is to go, they must be sacrificed without hesitation and without regret.

Listening

I am convinced that public prayers, both the written and the spontaneous, are "present" before they are received in the person who will speak them. On occasion, in informal settings, I have asked the Spirit or even asked aloud: "Who has the prayer?" People often assume I will pray because I am a minister. But ministers are not the only vessels the Spirit uses to hold and share public prayers.

---

[8]Blackwood, *Leading in Public Prayer,* 161–62. Here is Williamson's checklist for excellent prayers: corporateness, fervor, reasonable length, freshness of thought and language, concreteness, progression, expectancy, and dedication of life as the goal. Williamson adds: "Public prayer will not be effective unless it strives to move people to rededication of life" (Williamson, 28).

[9]Blackwood, *Leading in Public Prayer,* 169.

The ability to offer public prayer has to do, first, with the ability and willingness to listen. There are at least two levels of listening. There is an exterior kind of listening that involves being aware of other people, situations around us, and circumstances beyond our own. As God surely intended, ministers are magnets and people's stories iron filings. It is partly the impact of those shared and stored stories that softens the rigid protecting shells of our self-contained hearts, enabling us to listen again, and even more closely.

There is also an interior listening that must take place with some regularity. The first step toward it is finding a bit of distance from outside stimuli. It is not just that there is so much in this society to engage our eyes and ears, it is also that it is easy, very easy, to allow the constant engagement of our eyes and ears to become a habit. Some unnecessary stimulation is forced on us, other unnecessary stimulation is allowed by us, and even pursued. From time to time I am compelled to prescribe for myself a minimum of one hour per day of silence. I do not need to be motionless, but I do need to be television-, radio-, audio book-, music-, and conversation-less. A few days of this regimen never fails to bring me back to equilibrium.

The first stage of listening is hearing *ourselves* out. In silence, thoughts that are too gentle or tentative to push themselves in between ringing telephones and doorbells will surface and demand their due. With a bit more listening time, however, this work will complete itself, and the whispered comments of the trees, the quiet murmuring of the skies, and then, finally, the heaven-bound buzz of the prayers of the world can (almost) be heard. This is listening. I can get to this level quickly, without intervening steps, when I must. But I know better than to expect to dip living water out of a dry source. I try not to make a habit of "shortcutting" my way into deep listening.

Even though listening is hard work, I typically turn to it with a sense of relief. Anyone who does a lot of speaking must spend some reciprocal time listening. In the silence of listening, as the interior echo of my own words and thoughts begins to fall away and I tune in to the subliminal spiritual hum of the hopes and fears of others, I am reminded not just that I am God's, but that I am God's *child*.

It is with awe, then, that I revisit the vast, permeable, and ceaseless tapestry of prayer being lifted up all over the globe: within us, amongst us, below us, above us, and beyond us. The knowledge of that tapestry, a knowledge that is sure, refreshes my confidence in the Spirit's willingness to share prayer with me and in my ability to receive it and share it with others. Only after I have listened, clearing the mental decks of my personal issues and turning my face toward the task that is before me, can I begin to prepare.

Like preparing to preach, writing a prayer is a process that refuses to be rushed. I can do *something* in a hurry; I can do something in a moment, but I try not to lose the tenet that the children of God, and I, deserve my very best, and my very best takes time.

Preparing

One of the things ministry has given me is a profound appreciation for the remarkable human mind. Although I know almost no one who brags about the ability to remember things, I have found that tremendous volumes of an infinite variety of bits and pieces of *stuff* are stored up in most people's minds. If I did not have to "shake out the sack" so frequently, I would have little realization of just how much it is holding.

For example, in the late summer of 1996 I was working on a sermon under very painful circumstances. The Summer Olympics had come and gone from Atlanta, leaving behind a dull, back-to-normal residue of memorabilia auctions and departed-but-missed houseguests. My great-aunt, one of the dear and great role models of my life as well as an occasionally prickly but unfailingly accurate assessor of the world in general and my own ways in particular, had gone into the hospital in West Virginia with a mild heart attack. Both my sister and I called her when we received the news. Each of us was treated to her calm ninety-plus-year-old chirp assuring us that all was well. Within hours she suffered a massive stroke.

My sister, Linda, was already en route from Des Moines; I quickly followed from Atlanta. The news was not good. But at the hospital, holding vigil, I realized I was almost two separate people. One person was at bedside, in shock and in mourning, making awful life decisions with Linda and answering the gentle questions of family friends. Yet another aspect of my person was receiving a rare, precious, and long-hoped-for gift. A sermon that would be unlike any I had ever preached was taking shape in my mind. The occasion would be the rapidly approaching first Sunday at Spelman, when new students and their parents would fill the chapel. As I gathered up the historical background information I needed (I favor sermons with a historical twist) and exegeted the passage of scripture from Numbers, ideas and clarity of purpose began banking up in my mind like planes stacked up over O'Hare. I couldn't wait to dump the accumulating thoughts onto the page.

Frantically writing late one night, I came to a point when it was time to shift the focus of the sermon from the historical piece (the licensing of the first black woman to argue cases before the United States Supreme Court), to the scriptural piece (the argument of the daughters of the Old Testament Israelite Zelophehad; Zelophehad had died before he could receive the family's share of the promised land). Without missing a beat I introduced the daughters in this fashion: *Come now the daughters of Zelophehad*…It was bold, it was effective, but where had the language come from? I had no clue. Recently, I happened to be reading an old legal brief and noticed: *Now comes the defendant*…Apparently my previous career as a lawyer left some pieces in my sack I did not know were there.

I am convinced that ministers and others who speak frequently in public need to constantly add some things to their sacks while protecting their sacks from other things. First and foremost, I am serious about time with the scriptures. For me, it is not so much a matter of volume as intensity. I cherish the

Bible. The psalms are a favorite, but Isaiah and John, Job and Romans, Genesis and the Song of Solomon (!) intrigue me and teach me again and again. It is not just the Word, it is not just the words; the Bible is a way of being, a manner of perceiving, an angle of observing and considering that is true and straight and complete.

Devotional readings have meant a great deal to me at many stages in my faith journey. During my seminary days I read almost everything I could find on the movement of the Holy Spirit. That reading prepared me to receive the various miracles of life with confident joy. Catherine Marshall's books are meaningful to me, as are Martin Luther King, Jr.'s. The writings of Howard Thurman are of tremendous value. An immediate and continuing favorite is a slim and elegant volume of daily devotions, *A Guide to Prayer for All God's People.*[10]

Beyond that, I have poets—Gwendolyn Brooks and Maya Angelou are certainly two—who nourish my spirit and expand my focus. Author Toni Morrison intrigues me, Madeleine L'Engle restores me, and Derrick Bell challenges me. Lyrics are a treasure trove; Paul Simon writes great lyrics. The music of the group Sweet Honey in the Rock is wonderful (as are the women). Then there are the magnificent bits and pieces that are just floating out there for the listening, such as the song, "What a Wonderful World." It gives us, *The bright blessed day and the dark sacred night.* What a line!

Speeches can be very rich. Abraham Lincoln's speeches (and letters) are of a very fine quality. Bob Dole's speech upon his receiving the Presidential Medal of Freedom is a gem. Barbara Jordan left us with too few major speeches, but the ones she did leave are astonishing.

Andrew Blackwood called this "reading literature of the heart," adding that the foremost leaders in public prayer have

---

[10]Reuben P. Job and Norman Shawchuck, *A Guide to Prayer for All God's People* (Nashville: Upper Room Books, 1990).

been lovers of poetry.[11] Like him, I also read books of prayers. *Conversations with God*[12] is a favorite, as is W. E. B. DuBois' book *Prayers for Dark People.*[13] Ann Weems's combination of poetry in psalm-prayer form, *Psalms of Lament,*[14] has helped me to prepare myself for the grim business of holding memorials for deceased students.

Although I quote from the psalms regularly in public prayers, I do not always quote poems or lyrics or speeches. When I begin to know how I want people to feel during a prayer or how I want a prayer to be received, I will go to an author who invokes that feeling in me, read for a while, and soak my struggle for words in their successful effort. Then I trust them to lead me to the place where the words will be mine (ours) and appropriate to the situation and occasion, while the texture and flavor of the words are still theirs.

I leave room for the unorthodox but allow little room for the irreverent. As important as it is for me to fill my sack with fine writing and thinking, I believe it is equally important to avoid filling my sack with garbage. It is not just that many movies, television programs, and books are tacky and profane, they are also not very good. Because I speak a lot and frequently speak extemporaneously, I have accepted the fact that I must be careful about the material to which I expose myself. Much of what I read and hear will eventually come out of my mouth in some form or another. Therefore, I do my best to avoid "ingesting" material that will lead to inner stagnation or public embarrassment. Preparing for public prayer is a way of life.

Blackwood speaks of a preparation step for public prayer that he terms "sensing the needs of people."[15] For the pastoral

---

[11]Blackwood, *Leading in Public Prayer,* 117, 119.

[12]James Melvin Washington, ed., *Conversations with God: Two Centuries of Prayers by African Americans* (New York: HarperCollins, 1994).

[13]Herbert Aptheker, ed., *W. E. B. DuBois: Prayers for Dark People* (Amherst: University of Massachusetts Press, 1980).

[14]Ann Weems, *Psalms of Lament* (Louisville: Westminster John Knox Press, 1995).

[15]Blackwood, *Leading in Public Prayer,* 134.

prayers in chapel I am always aware of special needs and concerns. For campus prayers I have some sense of the issues and expectations. But for some of my public prayers I do not and will not know the people or their needs. Out in the community, responding to special invitations, I must settle myself by reading as much as can be sent to me in advance, asking the person who extended the invitation about the tone and intent of the event, and then relying on the Spirit.

Working

I seem to have what Bishop Edwin Holt Hughes encouraged in ministers: a "habit of the pen."[16] I write my prayers because I still hear in my mind the echo of the words of my theology professor in seminary, who entreated us not to "handle the business of the Lord with clumsy hands or clumsy lips." I can make allowance for nervousness, and I can make allowance for imperfection relating to the sheer volume of words I need to speak over the course of a worship service. But I cannot make allowance for poorly chosen words of corporate prayer when I had the time, opportunity, and ability to do better. Besides, I enjoy writing.

If I go to bed the night before an important prayer still in the midst of listening and preparing, it is not unusual for the Spirit to wake me in the quiet of early morning, asking: *Are you ready to receive what I have for you?* Those are truly sacred moments, and maybe a little comical also. My eyes filled with tears, my heart profoundly moved, my spirit focused on the words of thoughts or images being given, I fumble for pen and paper, calling out, "Hold on a minute! Let me get this down!"

The pattern of being awakened in the morning with a portion of the much-needed prayer or the next points for a sermon manifests itself frequently when I am tired. I don't write well when I'm quite tired, although I often continue to push and then have to discard the forced material later. It is

---

[16]Ibid., 147.

humbling and touching to be sent to bed like the over-tired child that I am, then to be awakened early in the morning with help before I can begin to worry about the day's outcome. God knows and acknowledges my physical limitations even when I do not.

A short invocation takes at least thirty minutes' working time. Invocations and benedictions for more formal settings take hours and on some levels, days. For Sunday morning prayers of the people (pastoral prayer), I briefly examine the morning paper and listen to the first fifteen minutes of *CBS Sunday Morning*[17] to determine intercessory prayer needs. Occasionally, a matter of national or international joy or concern will surface late on Saturday or early on Sunday and will need to be included in the prayers of the people. Prayers of the people usually take from thirty minutes to an hour to prepare.

With all written prayers, I work on paper for a while first and then work aloud. Some wordings that seem effective on paper reveal themselves as awkward or unclear when vocalized. I write prayers out in prose style rather than in paragraphs. I first became familiar with this style when reading Catherine Marshall's book *A Man Called Peter*.[18] In it she describes the struggle she had with the publisher of the sermons of her late husband, Peter Marshall. Peter Marshall had written his sermons in prose style for ease of delivery and to retain their rhythm, but the publisher was slow to perceive the need for printing them that same way. Catherine prevailed, and Peter Marshall's sermons were printed in prose style in his collected sermons, *Mr. Jones, Meet the Master*.[19] I have been using this style for prayers and sermons from the beginning.

---

[17] I tape the rest of the program and watch it when I come home from chapel. I consider it a wonderful program—informative, enlightening, and positive.

[18] Catherine Marshall, *A Man called Peter: The Story of Peter Marshall* (New York: McGraw Hill, 1951).

[19] Catherine Marshall, ed., *Mr. Jones, Meet the Master: Sermons and Prayers by Peter Marshall* (Old Tappan, N.J.: Fleming H. Revell Company, 1949). Actually, the style was originally suggested to Peter Marshall by Dr. Trevor Mordecai, pastor of First Presbyterian Church of Birmingham, Alabama. (Ibid., 17).

Readying

Once the prayer is written and I have read through it aloud until I am comfortable with it, I set it and my anxieties about it aside. I avoid eating immediately before delivering a public prayer unless the event includes a meal and my part is a benediction. I also avoid carbonated drinks. Sometimes I favor carrying my text on large note cards. On other occasions, I will tape the manuscript to the inside of a nice folder. I do not try to hide the fact that I am using a manuscript when I am in fact doing so. I make last-second changes to prayers at times and am careful not to rush those bits when I come to them. I try to mark the changes in the notes afterward, so the manuscript will be accurate as I file it away.

I do not memorize prayers in order to avoid carrying notes. With benedictions, I will memorize the portions of the prayer during which I would like to make eye contact. This adds significantly to the impact of the benediction.

I keep a tissue or handkerchief somewhere near at hand when I am delivering prayer; I am no longer surprised to be moved in its midst. When I come to the microphone or podium or designated spot, I pause, look at the people, smile, and open my folder in a leisurely fashion. There is a boldness to this, an unapologetic joy that makes the experience more satisfying for me.

If I am going directly into prayer, I use the classic *Let us pray*. After I have said this, I wait a few seconds until all (servers included) are aware that I mean business. Those few seconds of waiting (and it is not easy to do so!) make all the difference in the world in the effectiveness of prayer in "secular" settings and circumstances. In one of her novels, Madeleine L'Engle speaks of a musician's waiting until the music has fully entered her to begin to play.[20] I wait (within reason) until the peace of God has fully entered into the space, whatever the space, to begin to pray.

---

[20]Madeleine L'Engle, *A Severed Wasp* (New York: Farrar, Straus, Giroux, 1982), 388.

Sometimes I let a short poem , quotation, or scripture "pave" or "lead" the way into prayer. Using introductory words is as effective as using "Let us pray" and waiting. When people expect me to start praying and instead I begin speaking to them, they quiet themselves in order to hear what I'm up to.

Time and experience have taught me that if I make my concentration complete at the beginning, before the prayer, that concentration will almost certainly remain intact and screen out most distractions that arise during the prayer. However, if I begin before I am fully ready, my bubble of concentration is fragile and may fail me. When it does, if it does, I may bobble or swallow a word, skip a word or words, or simply fail to project all of the meaning of each and every portion of the prayer. This is not a disaster, but it is worth avoiding.

As I perceive it, in order for public prayer to be effective, especially in non-worship settings, I must carry the formality, the reverence, and the strength of the church on my person— in my manner and approach, in my attitude and look. If people have requested a sacred moment, a sacred moment is what they are going to get. I will not be rushed. I will not allow the moment to be compromised with inappropriate background music. I will not pretend to be doing something other than what I am doing, nor will I try to "soften the blow" by playing or joking my way to the task at hand. I smile because I am joyful about my faith and am always pleased to be asked to offer prayer. But I make it clear that the sacred moment is to be taken seriously by everyone, faithful or not.

Firmly opinionated as I am about all of this, I am also aware of the need to "woo" the people even as I dictate terms to them. Through the tone we take and the words we use in prayer we can make things harder on ourselves or easier. Both Blackwood and Williamson remind pray-ers not to "preach" their prayers.[21] They also warn pray-ers not to stray too far in the other direction and use the public prayer as an opportunity

---

[21]Williamson, *Effective Public Prayer*, 165.

to conduct personal devotions aloud and with a captive audience.

What is needed in public prayer is a fine and judicious walk down the center of the path. Shun the "me" thinking and the "you" language and embrace the "we" terminology and attitude. We are the leaders, yes, but "we" are also the followers, for we are being led by the Spirit of God. Just as with any good shepherd, a gentle but firm touch is warranted: "The speaking tones should be quiet and clear, never vehement and boisterous. The voice as well as the words should express devotion, reverence, surrender."[22]

In the bringing of public prayer in secular settings, the leader is the only recognized and acknowledged carrier of the good news of Jesus Christ who gets to share that news during the course of the event. There are other Christians present, surely, absolutely, but they will not be presenting their faith to the entire group. Just as surely, just as absolutely, there are people present who have parted from the faith, some who never had the faith, some who are struggling with the faith, and some who are wondering about the faith. Our bit of Christianity in spoken form is but one measure of sacred yeast in the secular dough of the overall affair, but, as we well know, one measure of yeast can leaven the whole loaf.[23]

> In the light of God's revealed truth, under the guidance of the Holy Spirit, a leader in public prayer ought to have a heart full of sacred fire that refuses to stay hidden. In the House of Prayer [and out of it] this living flame ought to set other hearts afire for God.[24]

What is said *before* the prayer in the attitude and style of the pray-er, and what is said *in* the prayer, will constitute the whole body of information for some people who may, in fact,

---

[22]Ibid., 20.
[23]Matthew 13:33; Luke 13:21; 1 Corinthians 5:6.
[24]Blackwood, *Leading in Public Prayer,* 20. Words in brackets were added.

be seeking some good news. No, this is not an appropriate occasion at which to say *or act as if* Christianity is authoritarian or judgmental and Christians are haughty or members of an exclusive club. Yes, this is an appropriate occasion at which to say by our demeanor, our warmth, the degree of our preparation, and the meaningful nature of the words we have chosen that God is worthy to be praised and that Christianity is serious, joyful, and surprising. And, yes, it can be done.

4

Designing Prayer Openings

Take with you words,
and turn to the LORD.[1]

If ever there was a person in need of orientation to a new situation, that person was I, in need of orientation to the experience of attending seminary. I had so much to learn, it is a good thing that neither I nor the instructors realized just how far I would have to travel. Or perhaps they knew; if they did, blessedly, they were too gracious to tell me.

On our first afternoon we were shown a videotape of Howard Thurman lecturing at Howard University. On the tape, Thurman, the famed African American theologian and spiritualist, aged and radiating dignity, calm, and wisdom, stepped to the microphone and captured the entire assembly (including us) with a look. Then he began speaking in a slow and thoughtful manner, finding and sharing the full meaning and scope of every word and phrase. His eyebrows lifted in awe

---

[1]Hosea 14:2 (KJV).

and amazement as he began: *O LORD, Thou hast searched me, and known me.*

I was mesmerized, enthralled, enraptured. I had witnessed mighty sermons, surely, but I had never seen anyone place himself in a position of such profound depth of spirit and apparent emotion before a lecture assemblage. As Thurman continued, I began frantically making notes—trying to take down the words, trying to take down their meaning, trying to take down the degree to which Thurman infused the whole experience with light and power. Other new students sitting nearby must have wondered what I was doing. For, indeed, I was ignorant enough of the Bible (and Thurman) that I did not realize Thurman was reciting Psalm 139 and that Psalm 139 was widely known as "his" psalm. Thurman was opening his lecture by mining the spiritual river for nuggets with some emotional impact for him, so that a similar response might be invoked in us. He was acknowledging and honoring the role of authentic emotion in involving and moving people.

The Bible is not coy, nor is it inert. The living and powerful Word of God has an age-old gift for waiting for, and then *claiming,* people. The Word waits for us to cast a moment of time, a hint of hesitating approach in the direction of those chapters, those books, those psalms and stories, and at the first bare instant of interest on our part (no matter how casually we intend it) God responds. The Word *owns* us in an actuality of possession that predates our conception and quite possibly predates creation. As Psalm 139 would agree, "such knowledge is too wonderful for [us]; it is high, [we] cannot attain unto it."[2]

What we are allowed, even invited to attain, however, is the understanding that there are portions of the Bible—verses, stories, phrases, psalms—that are *ours* just as surely as we are theirs. I have never known anyone to read the Bible with any amount of care or search through it for any amount of time

---

[2]Psalm 139:6 (KJV).

without finding contained therein some passages that speak to them specially and personally, offering both comfort and challenge. There is a verse in Psalm 139 in which the psalmist says of God: *Thou hast possessed my reins.*[3] Our special scriptures "possess *our* reins," including and particularly our emotional reins.

Those who lead in prayer need to know which portions of the Bible are "theirs." Obviously, we do not limit ourselves to using only those portions in public prayers. Indeed, some of our portions will be used only in personal devotion and will never be used in public prayer. But surely there must be, for every person who prays for others, a scripture or two that is right and appropriate for public prayer. For Thurman it was, *O Lord, Thou hast searched me and known me.* For the pastor who ordained me it was, *Giver of every good and perfect gift,*[4] and *God in Whom "we live and move and have our being."*[5] For me it is:

> [O] Lord you have been our
> dwelling place in all generations.
> Before the mountains were,
> or ever you had formed the
> earth and the world, from everlasting
> to everlasting, you are God.[6]

I can roam far and wide, using varied and occasionally creative openings to prayers, but from time to time I come home to my touchstone just as Thurman did and just as you must. This, to my way of thinking, is one of the keys of designing prayers. Allow yourself the infinite variations of approach and orientation, but keep for yourself a scriptural touchstone that generates strong emotion in you. Allow "your" portions of the Word to anchor you tightly in that original and divine

---

[3]Psalm 139:13 (KJV).
[4]"Every good gift and every perfect gift is from above, and cometh down from the Father of lights, with whom is no variableness, neither shadow of turning" (Jas. 1:17, KJV.).
[5]Acts 17:28.
[6]Psalm 90:1–2.

intent that you eventually would, and do, stand before others and pray.

In addition to needing authentic emotion and an emotion-generating aspect, public prayer needs to flow. The emotion is the content or the substance, but the flow is the means through which that substance is communicated. Opinions differ as to whether emotion generates flow or the reverse. It is agreed that the two assist each other:

> Emotion in prayer normally expresses itself in words that flow. In such onward motion they assume the form of sentences. Within each paragraph the sentences keep flowing in the same direction, with clauses more or less alike, resembling waves that keep tumbling up on the beach, until at last they reach their crest, when the movement subsides, but does not cease. Perhaps unfortunately, a love of rhythmical prose must be caught; it cannot be taught.[7]

For many of us, the issue relating to prayers that flow is not whether we love them or appreciate them, but whether we can create them. The good news is that if a prayer is begun with flow, with some encouragement the rest of the prayer will assume a similar pattern. Dual importance is placed on the prayer's opening then. It must bring the (often diverse) group of listener/pray-ers into prayer together, and it must set up enough momentum, or flow, to make listening preferable to daydreaming or rustling as the group moves into the body of the prayer. If a flowing rhythm can be established in the opening, that rhythm will help the body of the prayer to write itself and will help the listener/pray-ers commit themselves to the experience.

Flow can be "borrowed." There are already groups of words that, when strung together, cannot help but flow.

---

[7]Robert L. Williamson, *Effective Public Prayer* (Nashville: Broadman Press, 1960), 167.

We do not come empty-handed to the question of how a prayer should be designed. We come already holding a sense of the prayer, its essential element, its "door." Also, we have a mental list of what needs to be covered. The purpose needs to be blessed; the group needs to be blessed; any honorees must be blessed; and any food being consumed should also be blessed. If we know the group well, we may also be aware of special needs and seasonal concerns as well as thanksgiving that should be lifted.

In his book *Leading in Prayer*, Hughes Oliphant Old provides a list of the elements of a proper prayer for Christian worship. They are:

A. The naming of God
B. The hallowing of God's name
C. Claiming the promise of Jesus
D. Claiming God as ours
E. Seeking the inspiration of the Holy Spirit
F. Sealing the prayer in Jesus' name, who represents the Trinity[8]

As I perceive it (and will admit to perceiving a little differently than Old), the elements appear in this arrangement:

In the opening of the prayer:

A. The naming of God
B. The hallowing of God's name
C. Claiming the promise of Jesus
D. Claiming God as ours

In the acts of preparing for, writing, and delivering the prayer:

E. Seeking the inspiration of the Holy Spirit

And in the closing of the prayer:

---

[8]Hughes Oliphant Old, *Leading in Prayer: A Workbook for Worship* (Grand Rapids, Mich.: Eerdmans, 1995), 12–13.

F. Sealing the prayer in Jesus' name, who represents the
   Trinity

Although non-worship, interfaith prayer will deviate some-
what from Old's model, the essential aspects of his approach
can be retained. Some of Old's elements become even more
important in non-worship settings.

In the worship setting, prayer takes place in a sacred space
and is upheld both before and after by other sacred elements—
music, perhaps, or scripture. In all these, God is addressed directly
or indirectly; prayer is another instance of that. In a non-worship,
truly secular setting, however, because the prayer stands alone
as the sacred piece, bolder, more descriptive, and more exten-
sive language is appropriate. There is a need to "catch" the
people quickly and to bring them along with earnest dispatch.
Putting it simply, more ground must be covered in the opening language of public, non-worship prayers.

The classic and perfect example of a prayer opening that
fulfills Old's A, B, C, and D items and provides the model for
his elements is, of course, the Lord's Prayer:

D. Claiming God as ours
   Our
A. The naming of God
   Father
C. Claiming the promise of Jesus
   Who art in heaven
B. The hallowing of God's name
   Hallowed be thy name...

The A element, **the naming of God**, rightly insists that
prayer must be *addressed to* God. We, ourselves, respond differently when someone addresses us by name rather than just
throwing forth a thought or comment and waiting to see if we
respond. Many of us have had the experience of a public prayer
that just starts, but never does call upon God's holy name. We
have had that experience and would prefer not to repeat it.

There is a pointedness, a focus, to using a salutatory name. Therefore, prayer needs to open with one (or more) of many glorious and gorgeous names of God.[9]

For Christians, part of the reason God has many words of identification is because of who God is. God is ultimate (omnipotent, omniscient, omnipresent)[10] and everlasting, without beginning or end; God carries all that *definitiveness*. God is the power source and physical embodiment of all goodness (such as truth and light and wisdom); God carries all that *divinity*. God has to God's credit countless acts of loving-kindness, mercy, and miracle. God is still in the midst of doing marvelous things and promises a future of justice and blessing; God carries all that *activity*.

The B element represents both challenge and opportunity for the pray-er. How might we, how might anyone, **hallow**, honor, consecrate, or "make holy" **God's name**? Actually, there are several means of accomplishing this. First, we reserve the ultimate act of receiving prayer to God. We do not pray to anyone or anything else. This is part of the reason why "unaddressed" prayers rattle believers so badly. Praying to the ceiling or the occasion or the idea of prayer is a violation of what we hold dear and holy. We hallow God's name by holding the act of prayer exclusively to God.

Second, we reserve the language that describes God for God. We do not speak of any other entity as we speak of God. We may reference the spirit of truth or justice that has been made manifest in the life and spirit of a particular person or organization or effort, but we are careful to identify the original source of that quality as God.

Third, we are careful to give God the glory. The Bible's many references to "the glory of God," combined with our

---

[9]Actually, there's more. The Bible is filled with examples of persons' being asked, or invited, to call upon God *by name*. Psalm 7:17: "I will praise the LORD according to his righteousness: and will sing praise *to the name of the LORD* most high" (KJV).

[10]All-powerful, all-wise, all-present.

understanding that, despite our efforts, we fall short of this glory,[11] has led us to realize that not only is glory *of God*, glory *is God's* and is not our own. Therefore, we hallow God's name by crediting glorious acts and intentions appropriately—as originating in and flowing from God. This becomes very important in celebratory prayers. Some people do wonderful things, some people *are* wonderful, and this is to be celebrated. But those wonderful intentions, qualities, and acts originated in God, and it was celestial power that augmented and encouraged the terrestrial effort, bringing about the victory. In the light of God's definitiveness, God's divinity, and God's activity, we (are allowed to) name God.

In non-worship setting prayer, particularly, the C element, **claiming the promises of Jesus**, may be acted out and acted on by the pray-er while not necessarily being spoken in the prayer. The act of public prayer itself issues forth in authentic reliance on Jesus' promises. All that is required is for one other Christian to be present, *"for where two or three are gathered together in my name, there am I in the midst of them."*[12] The public pray-er relies on Jesus' promise: *"Lo, I am with you alway, even unto the end of the world."*[13] Public prayer is truly a manifestation of *"Ask, and it shall be given you, seek and ye shall find, knock, and it shall be opened unto you."*[14] More subtly, apparent to the pray-er but not always to the listener-participants, public prayer is *"Seek ye first the kingdom of God, and God's righteousness, and all these things shall be added unto you."*[15]

Whereas the shadings of element C may be subtle, element D, **claiming God as ours**, should be undertaken with vigor in the making of public prayer. Element D assumes an earth-heaven, "Jesus is mine" relationship, with Jesus' blood

---

[11]"For all have sinned, and come short of the glory of God" (Rom. 3:23).
[12]Matthew 18:20 (KJV).
[13]Matthew 28:20 (KJV).
[14]Matthew 7:7 (KJV).
[15]Matthew 6:33 (KJV).

acting as the bridge between us and God's throne. Even if that relationship is recognized by the prayer leader only, it is operative for the group in terms of the issuing of prayer and the receipt of that prayer by God.

In public prayer, "claiming God as ours" is the authority within which the act takes place. Christians have, in Christ, authority to act and ask on behalf of whatever assorted others may be present in a given place, time, and situation. This is part of our response to God. God is ours only because God freely assumes this responsibility toward us and makes it possible in Jesus. Nevertheless, God has made a commitment to us—not a contingency, but a promise.

Element A, then, the naming of God, has to do with who (and how) God is: God is definitive, God is divine. Element B, the hallowing of God's name, has to do with what God does: God is active as only God can be. Element C, claiming Jesus' promises, is the act of prayer; prayer gains its power and significance from Jesus' promises that we will be heard. And element D, claiming God as ours, is the heaven-to-earth lightning strike of public prayer in which those who have thought about it and those who have not, those who believe and those who resist, those who are in the mood for prayer and those who don't know there is a mood for prayer are brought together, gently but firmly, in God's understanding presence.

Elements A and B "speak" in the prayer; elements C and D undergird the prayer and give it its sacredness. Let us return to elements A and B:

Element A—The naming of God
Who (and how) God is

God is definitive.
God is divine.

and

Element B—The hallowing of God's name
What God does (and what we do in response to God)

> God did act, does act, and shall act.
> *Therefore*, prayer is reserved for God.
> God's descriptive language is reserved for God.
> Glory is reserved for God.

We can simplify this, and probably should, because public prayer commands not the theological process we have just undergone, but the results of that process.[16] We can paraphrase this into:

Element A—The naming and describing of God, or
Attributes

and

Element B— The hallowing of God's name, or
Activities

Thus, one very effective approach to opening a public prayer is with God's attributes and activities.

Prayer Openings with Attributes and Activities

In non-worship setting prayers, some who are present may not be in the habit of pondering either *who and how* God is or *what* God does. They do not have readily at hand either the A element (the naming of God) or the B element (the hallowing of God's name).

With identifiably religious people we can assume that the mention of God also calls to mind God's mighty works. Thus, a pastoral prayer in chapel might begin:

O, Gracious God

We know everyone is on board, already thinking of ways in which God has been gracious to individuals and to the group.

---

[16]Like preaching and leading Bible study, public prayer needs to be backed up by a great deal of thought and care and work, not all of which does, or should, find its way into the final result.

However, non-worship setting prayer needs to provide more information, hopefully in elegant and eloquent fashion. One way to accomplish this is by pairing attributes (who and how God is) and activities (what God does):

> Almighty God (attribute)
>> Who dwells beyond and plans (activity)

This is an intentionally bold beginning, but there is another deliberate piece. Because for many people (especially those not in the habit of worship and prayer) God seems distant, the prayer opens with God being distant, just as expected. This is familiar territory for listener/pray-ers. But the leader is just getting started, and adds:

> Patient and caring God,
>> Who bends near and listens

Again, two purposes are served. The group is informed or reminded (depending on their background) that God cares; God cares that we are gathered and are coming in prayer. Purpose two: God is brought from that comfortable and familiar distance of *beyond* a little closer, to *near*. Then the *caring* element is emphasized by pointing out that God is listening. Can God do this? Yes, God can; God has already been identified as "almighty." Would God want to do this? Yes, God would; God has already been identified as "caring" and "patient." We are now set for the third A-B pairing:

> Unspeakably loving God,
>> Who abides within and enables—

We are now in prayer together. The group is together (taking leaps of faith as a group are wonderfully uniting), and God is with us where we are. In addition, quite a lot has already been said about the kind of God that God is.

Because the qualities and interventions of God are so vast and majestic, attribute-activity prayer openings allow room for a great deal of creativity. Attribute-activity openings have the

capacity to infuse the most ordinary and familiar things with
power and significance:

> O God of the rising sun
>
>   or
>
> O God of the sweet days of spring blossoms
>   and the sloshy days of spring rain

Attribute-activity openings also have the capacity to share
a little theology:

> O gracious and glorious God,
>   who fills our world with amazing wonders
>   and human need
>   and asks us to treat both the same—
> To look into the heart of that which gives us joy
>   and that which gives us pause
>   and know that You are present there...

And they can be a call to action:

> O God of the rising hope
>   that calls us from the slumber of isolation
>   and beckons us to gather
> Bringing our diverse gifts of experience and
>   knowledge in our hands...

Attribute-activity openings can be a means of tailoring a
prayer very closely to the people and the event. For example,
spring commencement and baccalaureate is also the time of
alumnae reunion at Spelman. The women gather from all over
the world. Their pleasure at being on the blue-and-white–
decorated[17] campus is apparent, and each looks forward to
visiting beloved Sisters Chapel, a large and attractive brick
building fronted by a portico with six pillars. In the afternoon
of the initial reunion day, they line up on either side of the
alumnae arch, a high, pretty, vine-and-flower–covered archway

---

[17]Pale blue and white are the school colors.

on the campus lawn. The graduating seniors leave the Class
Day services in the chapel, processing through the arch (which
is the mark of graduation at Spelman), and the alums greet
them as they come through. Black caps and gowns meet white
dresses in hugs and smiles. Here is the opening for the alumnae breakfast prayer in 1997:

> Gracious God,
>> from whom issues forth the call
>> that rings in the listening ears of the women
>>> of the six-pillared chapel and the green-
>>> growing arch
>>> and the promise made to blue-and-white
>> and beckons them back home to Spelman...

An invocation for the College Language Association provides another example of a "tailored" prayer opening:

> O gracious God,
>> Giver of all miracles of love,
>> including the love of language...

Alliteration is helpful in attribute-activity openings, although clarity should not be sacrificed in an effort to attain it.
Also, the prayer leader seeking an attribute-activity opening
should not shy away from the anthropomorphism of God.
Imagining God's vast "hands" over and beyond our tiny, lim-
ited ones does not make us respect God less; it helps us trust
God more. Put simply, the identification of attribute-activity
openings is not a scientific exercise. It is an imagination, exal-
tation, faith-and-love celebration. It is a chance for the prayer
leader to *testify*:

> God is mighty, miraculous, majestic, mysterious, and
> magnificent.
> God is glorious and gracious.
> God is patient, imponderable perfection.
> God is excellent.
> God walks, rises, plans, hopes.

God blows winds of change
    into the lives of the oppressed.

God…"sits high and looks low."
God…stretches out the breadth of the universe
    and sprinkles divine secrets among the stars.

God…gives babies their bounce,
    toddlers their tenacity,
        and children their charm.

God is a weaver of wonders
    and a maker of miracle days.
God inspires and enables, indwells and empowers.
God goes before us and after us.
God "makes a way out of no way."

God is great and God is good.
God is worthy to be praised.

Scriptural Openings

For other prayer openings, a portion of scripture may be requesting an airing. In some circumstances the scripture can lead the way without introduction, as my favorite, Psalm 90, does so well. Other texts may be paving the way for a tiny homily.

In 1994, a prayer was requested for a "topping out" ceremony to be held on campus. Topping out ceremonies, which are Scandinavian in origin, mark the setting of the highest girder or beam on a building under construction. It is a way of celebrating progress in between the groundbreaking and the dedication of the finished building. Words are spoken, and good wishes are clipped to an evergreen tree, which is then lifted (by crane in this instance!) to sit on the uppermost beam.

The building in question was the Camille Olivia Hanks Cosby Academic Center on campus, which was being made possible through an unprecedented gift from Bill and Camille

Cosby of $20 million. The scripture that was strongly request-
ing a place in the prayer was *"Except the* LORD *build the house,
they labor in vain that build it."*[18] Unhappily, the construction
had been marred by tragedy. During the work, a beam had
slipped and killed one of the workmen. The grief of his family,
the construction bosses, and the college's financial vice presi-
dent, all of whom had been in attendance at the funeral, was
still heavy on my heart. Yet it was a day for joy, a day of achieve-
ment, with Camille Cosby in attendance, gracious, smiling,
and awestruck with the rest of us.

There was a need to gather up all these pieces in prayer—
the amazing gift of funds for the building, the oh-so-impressive
construction job, the sacrifice of life, the tremendous diligence
of the architects, construction people, and financial vice presi-
dent, and the clear mark of God's hand on it all. There was a
need to honor and recognize the work of the people, but there
was also a need to usher it all, including the loss, into the Holy
Presence for acknowledgment and blessing. This is the opening:

> The psalmist reminds us
> > that unless God does the building,
> > the workpeople labor in vain.[19]
>
> Far from minimizing the human generosity and labor
> > and sacrifice
> > that is going into this structure
> > as it rises out of the grassy slope
> > and changes the way we are seen
> > > and see ourselves,
>
> The psalmist's words remind us of the Great Blessing—
> > that what we are able to conceive

---

[18]Psalm 127:1 (KJV).
[19]As you notice, the text was paraphrased.

and contribute
and create
Is all part of God's gift of life, and love.

Let us pray—

Commencement in 1994 was scheduled to take place in the Georgia Dome, a huge and gleefully secular space, a professional football stadium that would be divided up to hold the ceremony. The physical distance between the dais and the assembled families and friends would be vast, and the sound system would be booming. The invocation would be the first words spoken, immediately following the organ-led processional.

Awkward as all this would be, commencements always are blessed occasions of majesty and beauty, as the faculty and dais party stride forward in the many colors and cuts of academic regalia and, most importantly, the berobed students black-high-heel their way forward with lifted chins, straight spines, gorgeous smiles, and palpable pride and joy. What should the first words at the microphone be? Perhaps the words that would be in almost every heart would be best:

The psalmist has the words for afternoons like this:
Bless the LORD, O my soul:
    and all that is within me,
    bless God's holy name.
Bless the LORD, O my soul,
    and forget not all God's benefits.[20]

Let us pray—

Hymn Openings

Some people are blessed with marvelous singing voices that they use very effectively, singing their way into prayer. I am not one of them. I have actually sung a few lines in homilies or other circumstances when there was no way to avoid that

---

[20]Psalm 103:1 (KJV).

public embarrassment. Sometimes making sure people know the tune of something is more important than keeping concealed the fact that you have only enough voice to hum or hiccup your way from point a to point b.

Not being able to sing has not kept me from using spoken hymns as a means of opening the way to prayer. I will use hymns under two circumstances: if the lyrics are powerful and perfect for the situation, or if the hymn is so familiar that my speaking it rather than singing it will not rob it of its effectiveness.

The college was, on Founders Day in 1996, a great deal stronger as an institution than in 1881 when Sophia B. Packard and Harriet E. Giles stepped off a train with a dream of starting a small school for freed colored women. The progress was miraculous but was also humbling. There is something about Founders Day that makes the college community acutely aware of its weakness and its utter dependence on God's guidance and mercy. Indeed, *"[God's] grace is sufficient for [us]: for [God's] strength is made perfect in [our] weakness."*[21] The prayer began this way:

> Guide us, O Thou great Jehovah,
> Pilgrims through this barren land;
> We are weak, but Thou art mighty;
> Hold us with Thy powerful hand…
> (adapted from *Chalice Hymnal,* 622)

> O most gracious and most glorious God—

In gatherings of African Americans in which the Negro national anthem, "Lift Every Voice and Sing," is not being sung, excerpts from that hymn, especially its extraordinary verse three, work very well:

> God of our weary years, God of our silent tears,
> Thou Who hast brought us thus far on the way;
> Thou Who hast by Thy might led us into the light,

---

[21]2 Corinthians 12:9 (KJV).

Keep us forever in the path, we pray…
(*Chalice Hymnal* 631)

To work well for prayer, hymns need to carry powerful imagery. Hymns that win worshipers through the grand swell of the music or through the simple elegance of the notes are sometimes not so forceful without that music (or those worshipers). To work well for prayer, especially non-worship prayer, hymns also need to operate out of a simple theology. Hymns that tell (or are based on) the story of Jesus' birth, life, crucifixion, resurrection, and our subsequent cleansing from sin contain too much theology for a banquet invocation. However, hymn language that expresses the simple truth of God's wonderful love can be shared to great advantage.

Sometimes it is not necessary to use the hymns themselves, but instead to reference the hymns or allow their titles to stand alone as places where we meet God. In this baccalaureate invocation opening (baccalaureate being held the day before commencement) the songs being referenced ranged from great hymns of the church through spirituals to gospel music. It might be hoped that every person would have some familiarity with at least one of the hymns.

O "Soon and Very Soon" God of the day before the
        day of…
O "Great Gettin' Up Morning" God of a Saturday
        made precious
        and permanent in our hearts;
O "Walk in Jerusalem" God, who makes us
        ready;
O "Sing the Wondrous Love" God, who makes
        us willing;
O "We've Come This Far By Faith" God, who
        makes us able.
            O Holy One—

Here is another:

O Gracious God, giver of that "Amazing Grace";
Unchanging One, who is the "Rock of Ages";
Close-at-hand friend, who brings that "Blessed
    Assurance"…

The attribute-activity component of the opening was also deliberate. God *gives,* "unchanging one" *is,* and "close at hand friend" *brings*.

Poetry, Prose, and Popular Song Openings

Poems can provide an excellent entrance into prayer. They work best in groups that share some common ground about a poet or subject. However, using poems, prose, and popular songs in prayers carries a caution: Consider with care the theology being expressed.

The group was first- and second- year students. The occasion was convocation, the traditional every-second-Thursday gathering in the chapel for announcements, music, prayer, and a speaker. The prayer opening was Sonia Sanchez's poem "A Poem of Praise." It was early in the year, at a point when homesick first-year students can use some extra reassurance that the adjustment to college life will not take forever and will be worthwhile. It was also a time when both first- and second- year students could use the reminder that they are special and blessed and loved. The students would not let just anyone tell them these things, but they would allow Sonia Sanchez, also black and female, to do so. Even for those who were not familiar with her or her work, the style of the poem was familiar and lyrical and gorgeous. The poem, used in this way, celebrated what the students were and what they were becoming.

Another entrance into prayer through poetry was at the dedication of the Maya Angelou Practice Theater, a special space that Maya Angelou had made possible in the Fine Arts Building with a generous gift. Debbie Allen's presence to christen the hall by leading a week of master classes gave the gray and rainy day sparkle. Illness kept Maya Angelou at home in North Carolina, but she was present in her poem "Just Like Job."

It is not unlikely that a piece of prose might "volunteer" itself as an entrance for prayer. Just as likely, someone requesting prayer might ask that a piece of prose be used. It is the task of the prayer leader to trim and rearrange the words, if necessary, in order to control the theological thrust and emphasis. For an invocation at an American Federation of the Blind dinner in Atlanta, the organizer brought the works of Helen Keller to my attention and asked that something be used. I carefully read through the materials he sent (her writings are *wonderful*) and then:

> Let us allow the words of the great American shero, Helen Keller, to lead us to the place of prayer...
>
> "I carry a magic light in my heart. Faith, the spiritual strong searchlight, illumines the way, and...I walk unafraid.[22] I believe that God is in me as the sun is in the color and fragrance of a flower—the Light in my darkness, the Voice in my silence."[23]
>
> Let us pray—

A Sweet Honey in the Rock song that was offering itself for the benediction at commencement presented the theological dilemma mentioned earlier. The song included the line, "You are the spirit of God." It was not so much that I disagreed, necessarily, as that I would not have described the role of Holy Spirit in that way. I am accustomed to and comfortable with "spirit-filled" or a person "having the Spirit come upon her." I probably would not have hesitated at "you *have* the spirit of God."

---

[22]Helen Keller, *The Open Door* (Garden City, N.Y.: Doubleday, 1902), 140.
[23]Ibid., 138–39.

Nevertheless, I liked the line because, in addition to fitting well with the rest of the lyric, it was surprisingly radical in a compelling, life-affirming way. It spoke directly and almost disturbingly about the imponderable value of every person, including the special young women poised and ready to make their marks in the world. It swept briskly past any shadings of questions or doubts about their marvelous *worth*. The very idea was rich with emotion.

What is the source of their life-spark? I thought during the listening stage before the preparation of the prayer. Where does their talent and intelligence, their personality and individuality find its original home? And is not the spark of life in them the Spirit of God in them? Eventually I decided to use the line unchanged. I did, however, change the group being addressed in the song from "we are" to "you are."

The baccalaureate speaker[24] the day before had preached a marvelous sermon about making your way forward in life. The sermon had three points: preparation, persistence, and purpose. Therefore, I borrowed from her first and then borrowed from Sweet Honey:

> Class of 1998:
> > in the vessels of your abilities, your training,
> > your background already present,
> > and the preparation, persistence, and purpose
> > > just now beginning to take hold in you,
> You carry the hungers and the hopes
> > of a people, a nation, and a world.

> But there's more:
> > As Sweet Honey in the Rock would put it—
> > > *You are your grandmothers' prayers,*
> > > *You are your grandfathers' dreamings,*

---

[24]The Reverend Dr. Vashti McKenzie from Payne Memorial A. M. E. Church in Baltimore, Maryland.

> *You are the breath of the Ancestors;*
> *You are the spirit of God.*[25]

Follow the path the Lord lights for you,
　　and all shall be well

And now, …

It is the opening of the prayer that sets it in motion, generating the upward-and-forward-traveling flow of spiritual energy. One of our tools for accomplishing this is emotion; indeed, emotion is one of the prayer leader's contributions to the process. Overly emotional prayers overwhelm the experience of prayer; unemotional prayers fail to unleash the power of prayer. Prayers that open with emotionally charged words are a reasonable and sincere response to the awe-inspiring nature of God.

Attribute-activity pairings and well-chosen scriptures, hymns, poetry, prose, and songs are words that cannot help but flow, and they bring their oh-so-reliable gift for rhythm and direction into our prayer openings. Emotionally charged words that flow into and over and around the listener/pray-ers cultivate interest on the part of the participants and urge them to listen in. The group is now ready to receive the body of the prayer.

---

[25]Language paraphrased from "We Are," words and music by Ysaye M. Barnwell © 1993; Barnwell Notes (BMI) from the song suite "Lessons," commissioned by *Redwood Cultural Work's New Spiritual Project*, funded by *Meet the Composer*. Recorded by Sweet Honey in the Rock on *Sacred Ground*.

5

The Body of the Prayer

Prayer, like everything else in God's universe,
is not accidental in its way of working.
It is based on laws—spiritual laws—
in their field just as constant and inexorable and fixed
as their companions in the natural realm.[1]

Experience in ministry has taught many of us that one of the few things that can turn a congenial group surly is asking them to make peace with silence. Pray-ers and preachers can bobble, mangle, and swallow words, reverse analogies, misquote and miscue, and drag crackling sheets of paper across a live microphone, but the one thing a group will never forget or forgive is being asked to sit in silence for an appreciable period of time. Consequently, worship leaders are inclined to handle silence with intense caution and hesitation, explaining with care when it is being used and cutting in half the number of

---

[1]Taken from *The Lost Secret* and quoted in Catherine Marshall, ed., *Mr. Jones, Meet the Master: Sermons and Prayers of Peter Marshall* (Old Tappan, N.J.: Fleming H. Revell Company 1949), 62.

seconds it is planned to be sustained. It is just as well; in church, ten seconds of silence feels like two minutes anyway.

Nevertheless, the appropriate transition from the prayer opening to the body of the prayer is silence. In the opening, the holy has been made almost tangible, and the gathered persons have been gifted with the astonishing news or reminder that they live and breathe in that holy presence and are in that presence at this moment. For believers it is an experience of faith fulfilled. For nonbelievers it is an experience of faith considered or at least tolerated. The preparation attended to with care, the focusing of the assembled spirits on Something beyond themselves, the carefully chosen words, and the call to and response from the Holy Spirit have combined to create a still and sacred moment that is the destination and intent of all the work and thought that has gone before. The group now stands in the doorway to intercession, and it must also stand in the wisdom of the psalmist: Be still and know that God is God.[2]

The prayer leader needs to keep in mind that while (s)he was thinking and listening and preparing, others were doing other things with no thought to the invocation or benediction. Once the prayer has been assigned to someone who is assumed to be competent and conscientious, no one else worries about it or even thinks about it until the pivotal moment. Moreover, the prayer opening itself may require quite a leap of imagination and spirit for the others assembled. They need a moment to settle themselves in the new realm, becoming more accustomed to the profundity of the moment. Whether the prayer opening is three words or one hundred and three, it should be allowed to rest with the people in the sacred instant of its own creation, surrounded and defined by its own moment of silence.

Those who speak more slowly can use longer pauses without artificiality. If the opening has been slow, the pause after the opening can comfortably stretch three or four seconds. Quicker paced openings allow pauses of only a second or two.

[2]Psalm 46:10.

Without regard for the length of the pause, it must not be omitted. The pause is the place-time in which the gathered spirits draw breath and collect energies for the body of the prayer; it is vital.

Praying about Ourselves

The opening of the prayer is about God. The body of the prayer is about us in relationship to God. God is always present with us, and we are always present in God, so prayer does not serve the function of bringing us together. Prayer does, however, serve the purpose of restoring us to the awareness of God's presence with us and our presence in God. Therefore, as we move past the sacred silence and into the body of the prayer, we augment the sense of God's nearness that we gained in the opening with the sense of ourselves, children of God *as perceived in God's light.*

No matter how "good" we perceive ourselves to be in our day-to-day dealings and contacts, the light of God's countenance reveals another, less flattering image. In God's light, we realize that our very best acts, thoughts, and deeds are but slim shadows of true greatness, that our wisdom is foolishness, and that what little power we have is borrowed, temporary, and weak. Public prayer, therefore, is not instructions; it is a request. As the prayer leader moves into the body of the prayer, it is important to recalll that all that follows is an entreaty and not an order. This perspective must be evident in the attitude, the words, and the tone of the pray-er.

The prayer opening is adoration, and in it God's holiness is proclaimed. This is the "A" of our acrostic, ACTS. In public prayer, the "C," confession, is often, and appropriately, omitted. Because the group is not a congregation and has not made a Christian commitment *as a group,* it is not appropriate to lead them in a confession. Absent the confession and in the absence of a broad sense of the need to celebrate God's forgiveness of sin, a declaration of pardon is also inappropriate, so that version of a "T," thanksgiving, would not be correct. However, public, non-worship prayers are an excellent time and place for a giving of thanks that is representative of the particular group. The body of the prayer, then, has two basic tasks before it—thanksgiving and supplication.

There is no enforceable rule that states that the A-T-S elements of public prayer must be presented in that order, or that elements cannot be dealt with at one point, then returned to later and dealt with again. However, clarity of communication, evenness of flow, and constancy of direction all favor some amount of precision in the presentation of the elements. Backtracking and repeating elements approaches the unhappy territory of the unprepared prayer. Moreover, the A-T-S order has a straightforward and natural appeal for us that may be a simple reflection of our Creator's preferences. In our dealings with others, even we children of God prefer first being addressed appropriately and then having our past efforts and kindnesses recognized before being asked to receive new entreaties. We like to be approached with decency and with planned and careful thought, and we like those who approach us to get to the point.

After the adoration and before moving to the thanksgiving, however, it is sometimes appropriate to spend a few moments in the doorway of the prayer before stepping inside to the body. In the opening of adoration and the sacred silence that follows it, the worldly shoes of the tongue have been unloosed and set aside. We are now on sacred ground and will approach the throne with tenderness, reverence, and care. Before we approach, it may be necessary to take a look around, endeavoring to perceive ourselves in our situation from this new perspective. For lack of a better term, this can be called "stilling." The point is to continue the concentrated and meditative direction begun in the opening. Stilling is a moment to revel in the "crossing over" just completed. It is not quite adoration; it is not quite thanksgiving. Stilling is our calm determination to set the ordinary aside for a moment in order to welcome the extraordinary. It is the reverence and awe that catches us as we pause at the threshold of an exquisite and long-sought place, gazing around and drinking it in before entering. Stilling has one foot in the world and the other foot in wonder.

The prayer opening that began with the Sonia Sanchez poem and was shared in the previous chapter was followed by a stilling:

> Gracious Creator of us all,
> We ask that you lift us
> > from the busy schedules we have all had
> > > these past several days.
> Settle our minds;
> > calm our hearts;
> > ease us away from all things which would
> > > distract us one by one
> > and draw us into a collective spirit
> > > concentrated on you…

Here is another example:

> We take just a holy moment this morning
> > to acknowledge this auditorium
> > and, indeed, this entire campus
> As one of your places of goodness and mercy…

A stilling is brief and transitional. Its role is to smooth the way into prayer by making note of the fact that a journey between two worlds is underway. Stilling can be important when people have come from all directions hurriedly and have had but a moment to settle themselves and gather their thoughts. Stilling can also be important in large gatherings that have just been brought from noisy conversation into quietude. Stilling may choose to acknowledge present circumstances (some of which may be operating against the prayer), but it also insists that the transition into a sense of sacredness will be successful. We are now ready to give thanks.

Assembling the List

Part of the reason for preparing public prayer is to assemble as complete a list as possible of those persons, items, and ideas

that need to be included in the prayer. It is not unusual to get
to the event and discover someone or something else that needs
to be in the prayer. If the basic list is not clearly in mind, the
last minute additions can tip the prayer leader over into fumbling and confusion.

Sometimes the person or group requesting the prayer will
specify what is to be prayed for. We do not expect those who
are not in the habit of offering public prayer to come to the
same theological understandings about such prayers that we
have. Therefore, the prayer leader should feel free to tailor or
adjust the points of the prayer as is necessary and appropriate.
The prayer leader also bears the responsibility for identifying
what is inappropriate and either deleting it or adjusting the
prayer to a more appropriate approach.

Sooner or later everyone who prays is asked to include
something in a prayer that should not be or is asked for prayer
over something that is not an appropriate subject for the kind
of prayer that is requested. The prayer leader needs to make
the requester aware when the prayer will depart substantially
from what was requested in case some discussion or explana-
tion is warranted or arrangements for a different prayer leader
have become necessary.

At times what is needed is simply for the prayer leader to
interpret the request and place it in a better light. I once heard
a prayer in which the leader, responding to the headlines of
the day, prayed for "those husbands whose wives cut off their
penises and throw them out of car windows." Needless to say,
that part of the prayer elicited gasps from the congregation.
The shiver of horror and titillation that went through the
prayer-participants is only one of the reasons the phrase should
have been revised or omitted. The other reasons are threefold.

First, the prayer was too specific and graphic to reach the
broader need that was represented in the news story. Indeed,
an appropriate entreaty could have been made—for the victims
and the perpetrators of domestic violence, for those who would
seek to have better relationships with their loved ones, or for
those who are struggling with anger. Also, the tone was far

removed from the reverent, humble, and careful tone that prayer requires. Finally, the prayer attracted attention away from God and toward the prayer leader; this is inappropriate.

> Not only must the prayer be grammatically proper, but the words themselves must be chosen so as to lend a mood of reverent restraint. If this is not done, the prayer may simply call attention to itself and thus turn the thoughts of the congregation from the prayer's main purpose.[3]

It is the task of the prayer leader to ensure that the group does not appear ridiculous or irreverent in the throne room of God. Indeed, it is the task of the prayer leader to bring all prayer to the heights and depths of what is important to God as we understand God. Good public prayer is familiar enough to resonate but not so familiar as to be mundane.[4]

People are important to God, so prayer leaders pray for all who are involved in or affected by problematic situations. Divine qualities such as truth, wisdom, loving-kindness, and justice are important to God, so it is always appropriate to pray that these qualities prevail. Moreover, when invited to offer public prayer, it is important not to think just of the persons involved but also of the cause or concern that is being represented. Offering prayer for trees or buildings may seem awkward, but newly planted trees can represent hope and celebrate God's goodness, and new (or old) buildings can represent God's faithfulness as well as the life journeys of individuals and institutions; these things can be lifted in prayer without hesitation. *It is not always the specific item or occasion that warrants prayer. It is the representation of the constancy of God's care that should be lifted with gratitude.*

In praying for organizations, the prayer leader needs to think of why the assembled members are involved in that organization, what it represents to them, and what their work may mean to others and to God. In honoring individuals, the

---

[3]Robert Williamson, *Effective Public Prayer* (Nashville: Broadman Press, 1960), 65.
[4]Ibid., 161.

prayer leader needs to couple the praising of achievements with gratitude to God for their gifts, made evident in the contributions for which they are being honored.

In blessing gatherings, the prayer leader should acknowledge the sincere investment of time and caring that made the event possible. And in blessing food, rather than ignoring the cooks in the kitchens hidden from view and the servers lurking around the edges of the event, the prayer can express the gratitude of the group by mentioning those who prepared and those who serve.

The point is to think *behind* the prayer list rather than only in it. If Miss Smith needs to be thanked for setting the tables, then "those who labored to prepare the occasion" can also be mentioned. If Ms. Jones is being honored, the people who work with her in her efforts might also receive a word. Remember, however, that exhaus*tive* prayers are exhaust*ing*. Some references must and should be broad. Old's element E, **seeking the inspiration of the Holy Spirit,** must come into play here. The prayer leader prepares the list of the body of the prayer and places it before the Lord not once, not twice, but at least three times. The Holy Spirit can be trusted to aid in the assembling (and editing) of an appropriate body of prayer.

If the prayer seems long and drawn out to the prayer leader during preparation, editing, combining, and condensing is called for. From time to time a prayer can toy with us, lurking in a loquacious land just shy of eloquence. At such times it may very well be that what is needed is not more, but less.[5] As Blackwood reminds us, the role of the body of prayer is supplication, in which the needs and desires of those present are voiced as petitions, and concerns for persons and circumstances beyond the group are expressed as intercessions. A few carefully

---

[5] Williamson considers excessive length to be the second most common fault in public prayers, the most common fault being lack of preparation. Included in Williamson's "errors" in public prayer are: lack of preparation, excessive length, poor delivery, monotonous reference to the deity, personal references, preaching disguised as prayer, and private rather than public prayer. His "excellencies" are: corporateness, fervor, reasonable length, freshness in thought and language, concreteness, progression, expectancy, and dedication of life as the goal. (Williamson, 7–29).

chosen words, spoken in measured and unhurried tones, can be extremely effective.

It is well worth the extra time it takes to seek out varied language for the supplications. Variety in language and approach keeps the body of the prayer from sounding like a laundry list and the prayer itself from seeming "last minute." Thus, it might have been enough to simply "bless" a new drama and dance practice hall, but it was more fun to ask:

> May words spoken, sung, and recited be clear;
> May steps danced be sure,
> and may the notes played here tell their own
> story.
> May the rhythms be sassy and syncopated…

You can "bless" the food, certainly, but you might also:

> … thank you for this luncheon, this abundance,
> Sustenance in a time of pleasant sharing,
> Yet another emblem of your merciful presence
> with us.

Or:

> May the luncheon be your nourishment
> for our bodies
> And the conversation and presentation
> nourishment for our minds and spirits…

The body of the prayer should be in character with the prayer opening, evidencing a similar style and mood. If the opening is simple and straightforward, the body should be also. If the body will contain some humor or a bit of play, a warm and friendly opening should be chosen rather than a lofty one. The mood needs to be consistent or, if it changes, there should be a transition to that change. When the prayer leader is clear about the purpose and the opportunity of the prayer, when (s)he has listened, prepared, worked, and readied with care, when the opening has been selected in true response to the Spirit's guiding, the body of the prayer will follow willingly.

6

Prayer Closings

There is a place of quiet rest,
Near to the heart of God,
A place where sin cannot molest
Near to the heart of God.

O Jesus, blest Redeemer,
Sent from the heart of God,
Hold us who wait before Thee
Near to the heart of God.

— Cleland B. McAfee

One Sunday early in my ministry, I preached a sermon in which I referred to paper origami cranes in an illustration. During the "slide-by"[1] that followed, I learned something about public speaking and private listening. A number of comments

---

[1] The "slide-by" is my buddy Yolanda's terminology for the exiting from worship, accepting or avoiding the pastor's handshake or hug, and saying or avoiding saying a word or two about the service. She points out accurately that some people and some Sundays deserve a "slide-by" option in which the parishioner simply leaves without contact and without comment.

were made about my sermon that Sunday; people were kind and trying to bolster the young pastor in her efforts to grow. Nevertheless, I noticed that three of the people (two adults and one young man) seemed to have heard different sermons. The two adults congratulated me for making points I had not made. The young man, who was in the youth group I was working with, handed me a paper crane folded out of his bulletin, gave me a big, public grin, and topped it with a big, public hug before drifting off to the refreshment table. He said nothing, but, in his way, he said everything. And what he said was far different from any other comment.

The lesson for me was that those who are present are not necessarily hearing what preachers (and pray-ers) are saying. Those who lead with words in sacred settings (and perhaps secular settings; I would not know) are sometimes victims and sometimes beneficiaries of the words themselves. That is to say, words may and will have meanings, paint pictures, and prompt hopes and memories for people about whom we know nothing. As we pray together, we are not literally together, because the journey of words prompts private flights of spirit in individuals in the group over which the pray-er has no control.

Therefore, it is probably too much for the pray-er to expect that every member of the group come along in the prayer at the same pace and in the same way. Chances are something has been said that has sent various ones off drifting, feeling, remembering. When you preach, you can sometimes see this. Some preachers fight it, others (myself included) do not. I can see people "leave," and I can see them "return," and I attribute this to the variety of needs that are being addressed. If I have said something about which they had to stop and think for a minute, was not that my intention in preaching?

With public prayer, however, it is more difficult to say where your group is as the prayer draws to its close. Even the occasional "um-hmm" and "thank you, Jesus" and "yes, Lord" common among African Americans receiving prayer do not necessarily promise that minds are not off journeying on their own. Prayer "talk-back" does not require prayer listening.

Therefore, prayer closings should never be perfunctory. As the tone and rhythm of language signals the prayer's end, the pray-er is restored to a status (s)he has not enjoyed since the "let us pray" at the beginning—everyone is listening and endeavoring as they listen to be in communion with one another. In those circumstances of united minds and hearts, the closing has three important jobs to perform.

First, the closing needs to continue the energy level of the prayer even as it completes the prayer. By all means, the care and sheer labor that go into the prayer should not be allowed to flag at the finish line. If the opening and body have done their work, victory is in sight. But there is still that last "kick" needed to bring the group over the finish line in style.

It should be kept in mind, however, that the closing cannot be expected to do all the work of the prayer. If the body of the prayer was not clear, was not eloquent, was not sufficient, the closing cannot save it. The pray-er is looking to finish up by "threading the needle"—finding a middle ground of reverent specificity, firm but not belligerent, exalted but not inflated, consistent with what has gone before, and deeply satisfying.

Second, just as the opening of the prayer carried us into a recollection of the majesty of God, the conclusion of the prayer should complete that circle by again visiting the throne room, but on our way out. As we go, we need a glimpse of *Immanuel reality*—a reminder that God goes with us. We do not leave alone or empty-handed.

Finally, the closing of the prayer needs to provide a way out of the moment of grace and glory. It needs to give us back to ourselves, to refocus our attentions on the matters at hand, and, perhaps, to remind us why we have gathered. It is a fortunate prayer leader indeed who is introduced well and simply and is thereby "set up" for the sacred moment. It is now time for the prayer leader to pass on the favor, "setting up" the rest of the program by leaving an atmosphere in which the program is right and relevant.

A prayer closing handled well, then, completes the circle made by the prayer and ties it up, gives the assembled group something to take with them, and restores the group to the time and place of the program. A wisp of remembered glory remains, but the group is ready to continue the event, made better by the experience of prayer.

It is important to remember not to rush this portion of the prayer. Time has been taken for a sacred moment already. There is no point in compromising the moment this late in the prayer by rushing its last few words.

The prayer closing can be perceived as having two parts. The first part is the clause or two that opens the door to the final words, the "pre-closing." The second part is the final words, Old's element F: sealing the prayer in Jesus' name. I consider the clause or two before the actual closing, the "pre-closing," to be a hand on the doorknob of the prayer. It is a signal to get ready, we are about to leave. Then, with the "in the name" language that follows, the prayer is completed and left to stand on its own.

Pre-Closings

The pre-closing must be in keeping with the substantial thrust of the body of the prayer. If we were talking about gratitude, it should also. If we were talking about seeking God's guidance, so should it. If we were speaking of our need to be brought together as a community and blessed as a body, the pre-closing can continue that effort:

> Bless us here and now;
> Bless us always and everywhere.

A good pre-closing and closing require that the prayer leader be clear about what he or she is hoping to accomplish through the act of prayer. He or she must *know* what sense it is that should be left lingering in the air after the amen. *Determining what sense the people should be left with may be an entire separate project in the prayer preparation.*

Returning to the UNICEF prayer referenced earlier, work was complete on the body of the prayer some hours in advance of the event, yet I continued to struggle. I knew there was one more level to which the prayer needed to go. There was no pre-closing prepared, and I had a sense that if I could figure out what it was I was trying to do, the pre-closing would write itself, complete the circle of the prayer, and allow me some peace in anticipation of the event.

Pondering this last piece of the prayer led me to ponder the point of the evening. Obviously, the UNICEF patrons were engaged in a good work. In fact, I admired them tremendously, partly because I had always admired UNICEF and had even harbored childhood hopes of working for the organization. As I thought about UNICEF, I thought about another group engaged in a similar good work: Marian Wright Edelman's Children's Defense Fund in Washington, D.C. As I mused about how blessed I was to have had the opportunity to pray for both organizations,[2] the pre-closing came to me quietly, and I received it with gladness. After a few minutes' fine-tuning, it was ready:

> May we walk ever and always
> In the gracious good company
> > of those who are friends
> > to the children of the world.

The question posed by the pre-closing seems simple, but finding the answer can be a serious journey. The question is: What last thing must we do before we depart from the throne room? What last word would God have us to hold in our hearts and hands and lift to the throne of grace before relinquishing this sacred moment? Sometimes we need an assurance of God's presence:

> And go before us, with us, around us, and within us
> > as we pray in the name of…

Sometimes we need a last bit of encouragement before embarking upon the task of listening to someone:

---

[2] A prayer for the dedication of the Marian Wright Edelman Center at Spelman appears in the chapter of prayers.

> Your people are gathered;
> Our hearts and minds are open;
> We are ready to receive
> And ready to be thankful to you
> In the receiving—

Sometimes we need a reminder that God hears all our prayers:

> In humility, yet in confidence
>   of your ever-listening ear, we pray...

Sometimes we need to acknowledge our blessings:

> Thank you, [Lord] [God];
> We are blessed.

to remember we are being led along the way:

> O Holy One of glory, lead on.

or that just being able to pray is a gift from on high:

> Accept this, our prayer, ...

or,

> This is the petition of our hearts
> Given in your name. Amen.

Closings

Old spoke to us about the need to close all prayers in the name of Jesus. It is the Christian understanding that Jesus asks us to pray all prayers in his name:

> And whatsoever ye shall ask in my name, that will I do,
> that the Father may be glorified in the Son. If ye shall
> ask any thing in my name, I will do it.[3]

Indeed, my sister, the good deacon, describes a prayer not closed in Jesus' name as being "like a letter without a stamp."

---

[3]John 14:13–14 (KJV).

In public, non-worship prayer where a variety of faiths are represented, however, prayer in Jesus' name can be perceived as excluding some of those who are present. Obviously, the Christian pray-er can press on without regard to this, but experience has suggested to me that people, especially those who did not ask to be prayed over in the first place, really appreciate any and all efforts we can make to acknowledge diversity and pray *inclusively*.

There is a very simple closing that accommodates Christians and non-Christians well:

(For) It is in your name we pray, [saying] Amen.

Christians understand that it is to Jesus and through Jesus we have been praying all along, so they recognize the prayer ending as appropriate. Others, coming to the seat of prayer from a different orientation, find in the closing a reference to the Divine. Closing in the name of the Divine is quite acceptable to them.

Some situations, however, call for different language. Perhaps the end of the prayer was very simple, and one more bit of elegance is called for. Perhaps there is a need to mention in the prayer closing that which was sought in the prayer. Perhaps there simply seems to be a need for a bit of creativity. These various impulses have led to the following:

In the name that is above all other names we pray;
In the name that means life and love, power and
    purpose to us all we pray;
In the name that stands glorious above all other names
    we pray;
We pray in the name that is above all other names,
    and fills our hearts with joy.

Or perhaps one of these:

Accept this, our prayer, in the name of the One who
    finds a home in holy righteousness. Amen.

> In the name of the One who knows us and loves us
> we pray. Amen.

This is not unlike the search for and celebration of God's attributes described in chapter 2. On occasion we are just having such a good time in the Lord that we cannot help but let it show.

The choice of closing language needs to be contingent on the pre-closing language. The important thing is not to try to do too much. The lofty language of prayer is gloriously habit-forming and glee-inducing. Too much of it, however, is counter-productive. Those receiving the prayer begin to perceive that the prayer leader is trying too hard, the language begins to call attention to itself (and away from God), and the reverent mood is shattered.

This is one of the reasons I believe in advance preparation of public prayer. In the office or the study, long before the invocation or benediction, is the best time and place to receive that pivotal reminder that less is more. This is also why speaking the prayer aloud is important. Only then are you ready to test out the acceptability of the prayer.

We pray because we are convinced that prayer makes a difference. Therefore, there is no occasion of prayer, no matter how mundane an appearance it may initially present, that is devoid of the life-giving, life-enhancing touch of the Godhead. Prayer has its power whether we prayer leaders grant it that power or not. Far better for us, however, that we allow the experience of leading others in prayer to lead us where we also need to be: near to the heart of God.

7

Prayers and Other
Seekings of the Sacred

Organization Events

In praying for organizations and groups, rather than imposing your assumption about their personality upon them, seek out the language they use to describe themselves. Be aware of the purpose of the event and their goals for it so that you can pray sincerely and in accord with the true concerns of the gathering. Also, there is no need to be intimidated. When you come bringing prayer, an encounter with ultimate might is about to take place. For example, a request for an awards dinner invocation received from a regional office of an organization concerned with the interests of the visually challenged might lead to a prayer like this:

Special Concern Organization Invocation[1]

Let us allow the words of the great American (s)hero, Helen
    Keller, to lead us to the place of prayer…

---

[1]Throughout the prayers in this chapter, I have used brackets and italics [*like this*] to show where each prayer must be adapted to its context.

"I carry a magic light in my heart. Faith, the spiritual strong
    searchlight, illumines the way, and…I walk unafraid.[2] I
    believe that God is in me as the sun is in the color and
    fragrance of a flower—the light in my darkness, the
    Voice in my silence."[3]

Let us pray:

O gracious and all-glorious God,
    in whose height and mystery we can worry that we
        are lost;
Patient and constant God,
    in whose depth and love we discover we are found,
Giver of gifts, architect of opportunities,
Joyful Creator of humankind in our marvelous
    and infinite variety,
Solid rock of divine intent, in whom we find our common
    ground,
It is with simple gladness and sincere lowliness of manner
That we pause in the midst of this long-anticipated evening
    of celebration and recognition
        to make a moment of sweet stillness
        in which we can thank you for our journey thus far
        and pray your blessings on that
        which is yet to be encountered and accomplished.

We thank you for the will of men and women and children
    to scale not just the low walls of life
        but also and especially the high cliffs of challenge.

We give thanks for the [*organization*]
    the countless stories of small victories and grand success
    and the fact that some of those stories are represented
    tonight
        in the vestibule, at the tables, in the program,
            and in the very spirit of this most purposeful
                evening.

---

[2]Helen Keller, *The Open Door* (Garden City, N.Y.: Doubleday, 1902), 140.
[3]Ibid., 138–39.

We give thanks, also, that the intriguingly good ideas, the
     gleeful energy,
  and quietly caring nature that you instilled in your child,
     [*Name*],
        even as you gave [*him or her*] life,
  found fertile ground and came to fruition in [*him or her*].
As we honor [*him or her*], we pray you to bless and keep *[him
or her]*
  and also [*his or her*] family and those who stand with [*him
or her*] in [*his or her*] mighty work.

Bless those who went before us to plan and prepare this day.
Bless the hands in the kitchen and those who serve.
Bless this food to the sustaining of our bodies
  and the content of this evening to the uplifting of
  our souls.

You are the delight in our tasting, the resonance in our
     hearing,
  the fascination in our smelling, the joy in our feeling…
    the One True Vision of our lives–[4]
And it is in your name we pray. Amen.

Prayer for an Awards Dinner of a Children's Organization

O God, you have been our dwelling place
  in all generations.
Before the mountains were brought forth, or you formed
  the earth and the world;
From everlasting to everlasting, you are God…[5]

O gracious God,
High holy One who crosses the height of the cosmos in a
     single thought,

---

[4]God is referenced as in each of our senses; vision is deliberately last.
[5]Psalm 90:1–2.

Yet leans low and close to breathe the breath of life
    into tiny babies as they are born,
Great Giver of gifts and the opportunities to put them to use
    in a needy and waiting world,
Loving Creator of those who gather in silken finery,
Loving Creator, also, of those who gather in nakedness
    and rags,

In the consecrated stillness of this sacred moment
We turn our hearts and minds to you
    as an act of gratitude
    and as supplication for continued strength.
We thank you for [*name of organization*],
    [*names of associated organizations*],
        their patient and capable leaders and workers,
    and all those who pause
        in the midst of the glories and struggles of their
        day-to-day lives
            to give thought and care for children.

We are grateful and do give thanks
    for [*name of individual awardee(s)*].
And help us to remember that although we honor [*him or
her*] tonight,
You honored [*him or her*] first: with an able mind,
        convincing voice, generous hands,
        willing feet, and a tender heart.

    [*Note: Keep God as the focal point of the prayer, not the
    awardee(s).*]

So we ask you to smile your joy onto this festive evening,
    then send us forth from it with renewed purpose
        and strength for the journey.

Bless all who organized and prepared for this occasion and
    tended to its details.
Bless the hands in the kitchen and the hands that serve.

Bless this food to our physical energies;
    And bless us, each one, as you find us—
        bowed of head and receptive of spirit.

    May we walk ever and always
    In the gracious good company
        of those who are friends to the children of the
        world.

It is in your name we pray. Amen.

Business Organization Luncheon Invocation

O Gracious God, who creates us
    not just to exist but to fulfill purposes
        both divine and intentional,
O high Holy One, who gathers us
    into communities in which we find our way
        to achievements
        we could not attain by ourselves,
O Almighty Originator, in whom
    our own lofty ideals of integrity and credibility
        are born,

As we call upon the awkward vehicle of spoken language
    to capture for ourselves a sacred moment
        in the midst of this busy day,
    We endeavor also to surrender a bit
        of our own authority and responsibility
            for the world
        in humble recognition of your omnipotence.

We turn to you in gratitude and celebration
    of these [#] successful years of the [————].
We thank you for the distinction of its leaders,
    reserving particular gratitude
        for [————], as [*he or she*] steps away from the
        position of [*chair*]

and asking special grace for [————] as [*she or he*] moves
into that pivotal role.
We thank you for new members
and for those whose long years of loyalty
are the cornerstones of the [————].
We ask that you continue to foster rich communication
and cooperation
among and between us all.

We lift our speaker, [————],
for your most generous blessing today
and ask that we receive fully
and with open-mindedness of intent
all that [*she or he*] will bring to this special occasion
of [*celebration, purpose-renewal, and strength-gathering*].[6]
As we turn to our meal, bless the hands in the kitchen,
those who serve,
and bless us as we share and receive
nourishment for our minds, bodies, and spirits.

And be our continuing vision, O God,
as we seek to hold fast to the paths of [*excellence, effectiveness,
honest inquiry, and civic responsibility*].[7]
As in your name we pray. Amen.

Mayor's Prayer Breakfast Invocation

Mayor's prayer breakfasts are about time. They are an effort to
take out some time (an everyday concept) to stand in the continu-
ity of time (a cosmic concept)—where past, present, and future
touch. Prayer breakfasts are a bold concept, and they warrant a
bold invocation. An interfaith approach is also required.

O high Holy One,
Grantor of gifts of time and place,

---

[6]This is a gentle rephrasing of the stated purpose of the meeting.
[7]This is a pared down version of the organization's mission statement. Not everyone
will recognize it, but some will, and they will appreciate it.

Seal of our past, fortitude of our present,
      Holder of the mysteries of that which is yet to come—

We are gathered today in [————], our city, our home,
    and a place in the uttermost of your love.
From [*date of founding*] until now,
    from before [*date of founding*]
        to beyond our furthest-reaching plans and ambitions
           for this city and its citizens,
You are our hope, you are our strength, you are our guide.

In the directed determination of this morning just begun
    we come to you
    seeking to avoid the paths ambition and wilfullness
        might forge for us
    and find, instead, your great intentions
        for our life together.
Young and old and in between,
From [*northern area*] to [*southern area*],
    [*eastern area*] to [*western area*],
    [*least mentioned area*] to [*most mentioned area*],
        hold us all in your tender care.

Divine purpose in our lives, you sit high and look low.
As we begin to address the issues of our day,
    [————]
    [————]
    [————]
        look upon us with favor and understanding
           and direct our decisions.
Bless the leadership of this city
    and all who labor publicly and privately for her benefit
        and good.
Bless this meal as we share it, and may it add to our strength.
And with that strength, may we serve you
    today and here,
    every day and everywhere.
As in your name we pray. Amen.

City Council Meeting

Unless the Lord guards the city,
    the guard keeps watch in vain.[8]

O Holy One,

With stilled thoughts and contrite hearts
    we come seeking your guidance this day, and your
        strength.
You know the many needs of this city,
    and you know our blessings as well.
We ask now for a sharing of your power,
    so that we can move confidently in this meeting
        and boldly employ our gifts
    to address the challenges of our times.

May our gathering today be marked by patience,
    careful listening, and a deep and abiding respect and
    affection for all of the people we serve.

May we stand for each other,
    may we stand for [*city*]
    may we stand *with* you.
As in your name we pray. Amen.

Corporate Partners Luncheon

Gracious God—
    From the innermost places of our spirits
    We give you thanks and all the glory
        for abiding with us and blessing us.
    You walk us along paths of purpose;
    You open portals of opportunity before us;
    You encourage our hearts.

---

[8]Psalm 127:1b.

[*Note: Those last three lines have a rhythm borrowed from
Psalm 23, verses 2–3a: "He maketh me to lie down in green
pastures; he leadeth me beside the still waters. He restoreth my
soul." (KJV)]*

We thank you for this [*company/institution/organization*]
   and those who work so selflessly
      to ensure a radiant future for [*our students/this city/this
         industry*].
From [*division or company at the beginning of the alphabet*]
   to [*division or company at the end of the alphabet*]
Our delight in working together for good continues to grow.
We offer it sincerely to you.

Be with us now as we journey forward in [*partnership/
   cooperation*].
Bless this food and those who have planned, prepared,
   [*and stand ready to serve it*], [*and have spread this table*]
   as we stand ready to serve you,
      returning thanks every day of our lives.

We pray in your name. Amen.

Sporting Event Invocation

Gracious God,
   We are met today on the playing field
      of your holy invitation to abundant life,
Giving thanks for all who labor on behalf of this league.
Asking your blessing for the fans who are here gathered
   and seeking safe and fair play and a good contest for all
      these athletes,
We invite you to be present with us here
   as we celebrate the life and the strength
      you have so generously granted us.

Please hear our prayer, for it is given in your name. Amen.

Date/Acquaintance Rape Convocation Benediction

When the subject is ugly and difficult, do not lose courage.

For God hath not given us the spirit of fear, but of power,
and of love, and of a sound mind.[9]

As the Spirit has invited, let us go forward in prayer:
O gracious God,
All-knowing One, who has anticipated the events
of these troubling times,
All-seeing One, who looks into the human heart
with both tenderness
and resoluteness of purpose,
All-holy One, who gives us free will while standing ready,
determined, and able
to infuse all of our steps toward goodness
with divine assistance
and clarity of direction,

We thank you for [*sponsoring group/the helping professionals*]
and those who work with them
and all who take matters of the mind and spirit
as their area of endeavor and effort.
We thank you for the way they stand with us all,
the constancy of their concern and care,
and the compassionate professionalism
of their guidance.

Continue, we pray, to share with them
your spirit of wisdom,
So that the pathway of their steps may always be lined
with the greater understanding, increasing strength,
and joy
that come from you through them to this community
of [*positive descriptive term for the community*].

---

[9]2 Timothy 1:7 (KJV).

We thank you for your presence here with us today,
And we ask that the seeds that have been scattered
    so firmly but gently this morning
    will fall on fertile ground and spring up into strength—
        now, if necessary; or in timely fashion,
        if ever necessary,
    so that no one need be a victim,
        and, most especially,
            no one need be a victimizer.

And now, dismiss us in your love, peace, and power.
Go before us and make straight our ways;
    Go behind us and redeem our days;
        Go with us as we praise you;
O Holy One of glory, lead on. Amen.

Association Conference Invocation

With conferences it is important to remember that people will have traveled over distances (sometimes with difficulty) and will be in an unfamiliar setting among strangers. The prayer can help settle the group into the space and the company of one another. If the prayer leader knows in advance that the invocation will be followed by the keynote address, praying for the speaker is natural and will be appreciated. Association prayers need not only to reflect but also to celebrate the belief system and interests of those who are gathered. Finally, the prayer should reflect the mood of the conference—the nature of what is being undertaken, its seriousness or lightness.

O God of the rising hope
    that calls us from the slumber of isolation
    and beckons us to gather,
        bringing our diverse gifts of experience
          and knowledge with us;

We come seeking your spirit of wisdom.

Your awareness of us, your human creation,
    lifts high, digs deep, and spreads wide.
So we need not list for your divine self
    the challenges we face as we stand at the gateway
        of this [*nature or name of the*] conference.
Instead, we stand back and ask you to enter first
    and lead us in [*nature of business*]
So all that we do these [*3*] days—
    and we pray that it will be profound—
Be worthy of this community of women and men
    and enjoy the guidance of your power.
Thank you for this assemblage—
    for those who have traveled over distances safely;
Thank you for the wealth of planning that has brought us to
        this day.
Thank you for [*the keynote speaker's name*] as [*he or she*] comes
    and for others who will follow.
Accept our appreciation for this moment
    to share in the Spirit,
    who bids us to see challenges
    and come seeking solutions.

In humility, in gratitude, and in your mighty name we pray.
Amen.

Sometimes you are dealing with conference organizers who become more and more harried each time you hear from them. They might appreciate a special word in the conference invocation:

Give the organizers and enablers of this conference
    the gift of your peace
    so that they might mingle with the people,
        perceive that all is well,
            and call the day a victory.

————————————*Children*————————————

Dedication of a Daycare Center

If the center is being named after someone, the person can be identified and his or her work be celebrated briefly either before the prayer or during it. This again points out the value of doing some research and being aware of the elements that go into the occasion. For example, in the dedication of a center being named after Marian Wright Edelman, her name and the work of her organization were used as an introduction to the prayer.

[*The Sabbath is the day on which work is brought to a pause*
   while worship and thanksgiving become the gathering place
      of body and spirit.
For many Christians the Sabbath is the first day of the week.

This is the first day of the first week
   of the Spelman College Nursery and Kindergarten made new
      as the Marian Wright Edelman Center;
So I am here to declare this Children's Sabbath in May,
   a worthy and ready day for pausing and praising
      and thanking God.

Marian Wright Edelman gave us the Children's Defense Fund,
   and the Children's Defense Fund gave us Children's Sabbath,
      along with a renewed sense of the treasury that is our
         children—]

Let us give our most prayerful selves to God.

   Most gracious and most glorious God,
   Who gives babies their bounce,
      toddlers their tenacity,
      children their charm,
      and grown-ups earthly responsibility for each and
         every one,

We thank you for this consecrated spot in the midst of
    [*wherever the center is located*],
  which continues to be set aside
    for the elevated voices,
      gleeful grins,
        endless explorations,
          and delightful growth of children.

A portion of the spirit of this [*city/community/campus*] resides
  here with them.

Bless the children of then and now and yet to be.
Bless their parents.
Bless their teachers, protectors, advocates, and namesake,
  for all are precious to us.
And may we who are here at [————]
    forever be decorated with drawings
    and smudged into clarity of direction
      by the tiny prints of children's hands.

In the name that is joy and promise, laughter, love, and hope
  we pray. Amen.

Prayer for the Opening of the Little League Season

Two needs are immediately apparent: The prayer needs to be interfaith, and it needs to be clear, brief, and straightforward because of the children.

Great and high Holy Creator—

We thank you for all who have worked and hoped and planned
  to bring us to the beginning of this, the[————]
    Little League season
    in the city of [————].
We ask you now to bless our players, our families,
  our coaches and umpires,

and the many friends and supporters who help make this
season a reality.

May we play well and happily,
with many new friendships being made within and
among the teams.
May we be kept from serious injury.
May we be graced with good weather,
and may the sodas be cold,
the pizzas [or *whatever the typical post-game treat is*] be
hot with extra cheese,
the grass be green,
and the joy of teamwork be great
all summer long.

As in your name we pray. Amen.

With this kind of prayer it would be good to mention team
names, if possible. If there are a large number of them, a few could
be selected based on their alphabetical order (from the Atoms to
the Zephyrs) or distance—from the furthest north to the furthest
south, from the furthest east to the furthest west. Team names
would fit in nicely just before the phrase, "May we play well and
happily..."

The Creative Arts

When the event is arts related, the art can be celebrated, with
God being identified as the creative force behind all that is made.
If an item or location is the subject of the event, a prayer of invocation at the dedication ceremony will need to be very different from
the prayer of dedication of the item (statue, painting, etc.) or location itself. Be a savvy prayer leader and, if possible, take a look at
the item (or room) and its location before sitting down to prepare.
If the event is music or dance, find out what is on the program
before preparing.

Statue Dedication Event Invocation

O gracious and loving Mother/Father/God,

With a thought you made us,
With a breath you gave us breath.
Your gift of life alone would have been enough;
>   but out of your greatness,
>   >   your loving-kindness,
>   >   >   your joy,
>   and your spirit of beauty and truth,
You open wide your celestial storehouse
And shower us with gifts of creation
>   so that we might use our voices, our words,
>   >   our bodies, our hands
>   >   >   in ways mysterious, satisfying,
>   >   >   >   and astonishing.

You set us free to fly, dear God, and we thank you.

So bless us as we gather,
>   as we pause to celebrate gifts
>   >   so evident among us.
We forget not to be grateful, also and ever
>   to the Giver.

In the name that is above all other names we pray. Amen.

Dedication of a Statue

From the heart of the psalmist these words are given:

>   Satisfy us, [*O God*], in the morning
>   >   with your steadfast love,
>   so that we may rejoice and be glad all our days.
>   Let the favor of the Lord our God [*or our Creator*] be
>   >   upon us,
>   >   and prosper for us the work of our hands,
>   >   O prosper the work of our hands![10]

---

[10]Psalm 90:14, 17.

Let us pray:

Transcendent God of the hunger to create,
Unspeakably masterful Holy One,
Author and finisher of accomplishment and creation,
    true home-heart of glorious gifts—

Receive us in victory today as heaven and earth touch
    and the work of the hands of [———] is established
        here in [———].
May this [*painting/sculpture/other*] continue to speak volumes
    to coming generations,
        even as it engages us today.

[*May it mark a special moment of truth and clarity of purpose
    on our long, long journey forward*] OR
[*May it celebrate the love and respect this institution has for (name)
    in a way that lifts us beyond this temporal space
    and places us in the hallowed halls
    where timeless truths echo softly.*]
And may this [*alcove/hall/garden*] be a place
    where artistry issues a welcome invitation
        to pause and be renewed,
        to reflect and be inspired.

We dedicate this [———] to each other;
    we dedicate it to all the hopes and dreams of
    [*this community/our people/*———];
    we dedicate it to you and all that you call us to be.

In remembrance, in acknowledgment,
    and in your name we pray. Amen.

Topping Out Ceremony Prayer

The lifting of the topmost girder onto a construction project is
sometimes celebrated with a Scandinavian ritual called a "topping-
out" ceremony. Prayers are prayed; words are spoken; good wishes

are tied to an evergreen tree; and the tree is lifted up to stand at
the top of the building, affirming life and representing the giving
of thanks. This prayer includes mention of a particular construction
worker who was killed while working on the building.

The psalmist reminds us
    that unless God does the building,
    the workpeople labor in vain.
Far from minimizing the human generosity
    and labor
    and sacrifice that is going into this structure
        as it rises out of the grassy slope
        and changes the way we are seen
                and see ourselves,
The psalmist's words remind us of the great blessing—
    that what we are able to conceive
        and contribute
        and create
            is all part of God's gift of life and love.

Let us pray:

From your hands, through our hands
    to this building taking shape before us,
We thank you, O God, for the gathering of generosity
    and creative talent,
    skill, patience, sweat, and sacrifice
        that have met on this campus.
At each step we have been caught up in awe and
        amazement.
The gift itself, the complex plans,
    the crater in red clay,
    the mighty machinery,
        and dedicated workpeople
All call forth our admiration and our profound appreciation.
Thanking you, we are also thanking all those who have built
    and are participating in the building;
        and we lift them for your blessing.

[*May the family of—————find not pain*
   but consolation in this structure.
His work, the work of all those gathered today,
   is a source of pride
      and will continue to inspire
         for many years to come.]
Keep us in your all-powerful hands
   as the work continues.
Give us safety, good weather, and the satisfaction
   of a job well done.
Look with pleasure upon our tree—
   an evergreen in an unlikely place.
Our hearts are ever aspiring upward,
   and our gratitude is ever yours.
In the name of the One who knows us and loves us, we pray.
Amen.

Dedication of a Practice Theater

In dedicating a facility, it is nice to take a peek into that facility's future in the midst of the prayer. Note these words from the dedication of a practice theatre:

May words spoken, sung, and recited be clear.
May steps danced be sure
   and the notes played tell their own story.
May the rhythms be sassy and syncopated.
May those yearning to polish their art
   and those who live to help in the polishing
      continue to meet within these walls.

Music Recital Invocation

O gracious and most holy God,

In humility, in simplicity, with quieted spirits
   and grateful hearts
      we turn to you now, in the listening silence of [*location*],
   seeking further consecration of this place
      for what is about to begin.

We ask that your gift of music be visited in our midst
       this [*time of day*]
    powerfully, mysteriously, and wonderfully.
We ask that you accept from these musicians' hands
    the long work and preparation they have invested
       in sharpening and honing their skills.
We ask that you take that investment, magnify it, glorify it,
    and carry it that extra celestial distance
       so that we might hear from you
       in the pieces that have been prepared.

Bless [*featured musicians*]
    and anoint [*her/him/them*] with your love, confidence,
       and joy.
Uplift the guest singers and players
    on lyrical waves like the wings of doves.
Combine their gifts in beauty
    and open our hearts to receive all that they have to give
       and all that you have to say through them.
Be with us, be in us, be the notes and the words,
    be the voices and the fingertips,
Then accept our thanks and our praise
As in your name we pray. Amen.

———————————*Not Quite Church*———————————

Not everyone is comfortable with the institutional church. Nevertheless, in times and circumstances of pain and trouble or other times when an uplift is needed, people may seek out rituals similar to those of the church as a source of consolation or inspiration. A representative of the church may be invited to come and offer prayer at such an event. Obviously, what is called for in such circumstances is a carefully assembled blending of the context of the church and the context of those who are performing the ritual.

When a tree-planting (or scholarship dedication or related event) is planned in honor of someone who has died, it is both a continuation of the grieving process and a hope for the beginning of healing. The prayer may need to visit both—recalling the deceased while, at the same time, gently moving the group on along life's path.

Invocation for a Tree-Planting Event

Dear, merciful, and gracious God,
　giver of all good and perfect gifts,
　loving home-heart of the eternal soul of [————],
　compassionate sustainer of [————'s] [*parents/children/co-
　　workers/teachers/friends*].

This is a day for honestly saying
　that we still spend time down on the bank
　　of the River Jordan,
　peering across and into the mysterious mist shrouding
　　the far side,
　hoping even yet to get just one more glimpse
　　of [————'s] earthly life
　　or a first glimpse of [*his or her*] eternal life.

We know [*she or he*] is loved in your arms, in your presence,
　in your places of joy and completeness;
But [*she or he*] is loved here also and missed and
　remembered.
[*Now take some time to repeat the qualities of the deceased.
　If the family and friends did not need to hear them, they
　would not have scheduled the event.*]

[————] was exceptional, that we cannot and will not deny.
So it is with deep measures of expectation
　that we wait to see what [*his or her*] legacy will be.
In [————], you did wonderful, delightful, marvelous things;
Through memories of [*him or her*], with our help,
　may there yet be additional achievements
　　and glories to celebrate.

Keep us faithful; keep us steadfast;
　keep us hoping in you.

Walk with us this day and in this consecrated hour
   in all consolation and with power.

As ever and always, we pray in your holy name. Amen.

Prayer of Dedication of a Tree

When a tree is being dedicated, it needs to be perceived and perhaps even described as more than a tree. The divine qualities, the eternal qualities of trees need to be lifted up. Also, a tree being dedicated is more than a symbol of life, of hope, of the cycle of birth and death and birth again. Put simply, it is a living thing to touch and watch when something (someone) we long to touch and watch is gone from our access. Dedicated trees are stand-ins for deceased loved ones.

Whether you use a quotation about trees as a lead-in or not, you can prepare the way toward a tree dedication by browsing through the "tree" entries in Bartlett's *Familiar Quotations*.[11] In addition, Isaiah 55:12 has a wonderful bit of tree imagery:

> For you shall go out in joy, and be led back in peace;
> The mountains and the hills before you shall burst
>   into song,
> And all the trees of the field shall clap their hands.

People are usually standing at tree dedication ceremonies. The prayer should be brief but deep.

O Holy One of love and purpose and plan,
Look upon us with patient understanding in this moment.
   Gather our hearts and minds
      to your radiant throne room
         and hear our prayer.

---

[11]John Bartlett and Justin Kaplan, eds., *Familiar Quotations: A Collection of Passages, Phrases, and Proverbs Traced to Their Sources in Ancient and Modern Literature*, 16th ed. (Boston: Little, Brown, 1992).

As in the fullness of your time
    the roots of this [*little*] [*maple/oak/pine*] begin to loosen
        and settle
    and find their way into the life-sustaining soil,
    please know that, like this tree, our memories and our
        hopes are planted here.

We cannot give up on love, and we do not.
Many waters cannot quench love,
Neither can floods drown it.[12]
    So, even when it hurts,
        even when it chills and burns,
We stake our claim in recalling [*name*].
We take sincere joy in honoring [*his or her*] life.
We plant this tree in [*name's*] name
    and trust you in your magnificent tenderness
        to give it increase.

Please accept this tree in the spirit in which we are
        struggling to give it.
Support and challenge it with wind.
Send your glorious freshets above it, then bring them down
        to it as rain.
Keep it company with beetles, butterflies, and birds.
    Smile your sun of righteousness down upon it
        and us
    that we might find healing and nurture in its wings.[13]

The growth of a tree,
    like the perfecting of a life,
Is a task best left to you.
Grow this tree into sky-seeking beauty
    as you make [*name's*] life perfect in your sight.

---

[12]Song of Solomon 8:7.
[13]This is a reference to Malachi 4:2: "But for you who revere my name the sun of righteousness shall rise, with healing in its wings."

We commit ourselves to giving you praise and glory
    season after season
        in spirit and in truth.

This is the petition of our hearts
    Given in your name. Amen.

Memorial Service

In preparing an invocation for a memorial service that would take place on the stage of a college drama and dance department and mark the deaths of several nationally and locally known women of the theater arts, my mind sorted through a mental catalog of nonchurch rituals until it came to a childhood story of an Asian ritual that included placing lighted candles on tiny paper boats and setting them adrift on the water by night. That provided the imagery for the opening of the prayer.

Take us to the water, O God,
Lead us to your shores
    so that we can stand in loving and honorable tribute
    as the spirits of our sister warriors are floated away
        from us
        on your river of time.

In each one of them you made a special investment of talent
    and gifts;
From each one of them we received your investment a
    thousandfold and more—

    [*Stories told and costumes that aided in the telling,*
    Acting and dance that made it all draw breath and live,
    Eloquence that melted old days and ways into empty
        husks and demanded that a new day be declared.]

So we thank you for who they were and what they did,
But also we praise you for who and what they refused to be
    and do.
Their passionate commitment to their arts, their vocations,
    their callings, and their truths

has paved our path with the strength of possibility,
edged our course with courage of self-respect,
and lit our journey with the incandescence of
    ability
        combined with tenacity
            and built into mastery.

Stand with us, if you would, then, O Creator and Friend.
Receive this celebration with tender hands and an
    understanding heart.
As our sister warriors were, please let us be—
    victorious in ourselves, yet fulfilled in you
As in your gracious name we pray. Amen.

Habitat for Humanity Home Groundbreaking

Except the LORD build the house, they labor in vain that
    build it.[14]

Loving, steadfast, and holy God,
    builder and sustainer of blessings not made by hands,

May it be in your almighty will, we pray,
    that the hope and vision,
        planning and efforts of your people
           converge truly on this spot.
Over the next [*days and weeks*]
    may our work together be a celebration
        of the way you invite us to care for one another.
We thank you for the many backs that will bear the burden
    of labor,
    the many hands that will execute the countless tasks,
    the many individuals and concerns
    who will share the vital supplies,
    and your celestial blueprint in which
    it all finds reality.

---

[14]Psalm 127:1a (KJV)

Bless us, if you would, with a safe job encouraged along by
    favorable weather.
And may the soon-to-be-homeowners, [————],
    see, as the progress continues and the structure rises,
        that what is being built is not a house, but a home.

Keep us building, keep us sharing, keep us trusting in you
As in your name we pray. Amen.

Habitat for Humanity Home Dedication

Gracious God of endless glory,
    divine heart's-home of life and love,
    spirit of faith, vision of victory,
        hearer of prayer,

We would not be here, indeed, we would not be gathered
    without your favor that brought us from
        [*homeowner's name(s)*]'s earliest hopes until now.
So this is a petition for your continued kindness.
May the caring service of those who helped turn this
        empty place
    into a glad address
    return to them as goodness in their lives.
May these new homeowners find security and peace
    and pleasant neighbors here.
May our gathering today become the first
    of what is needed to make a home special and right:
        memories of friends smiling their way in the front door.
Human hands built the building,
    but you built the blessing.
So it is in your name we pray. Amen.

Blessing of the Pins of New Nursing Graduates

It is important to consider and lift up not just the actual pins,
but also their symbolic importance. Rather than avoiding the physical nature of the objects, embrace it and allow it to prompt language and imagery in the prayer.

Gracious God of remembrance and anticipation,
of ability and continuing growth,
of life and death,

In your divine wisdom, please allow these pins
to be a symbol of our prayers for these nurses
as they go their way.

May the pins ever be put on with prayer
and removed with praise.
May they be worn with poise;
and where their wearers go, may you already be.
May these emblems of accomplishment and pride
be a welcome sight wherever they are touched and seen.
May the sharp and pointed tips on these back of these pins
remind their wearers daily
that it is within their capacity
to share and reduce all kinds of pain
if they are willing to work
with undaunted courage
and ultimate care.

May a blessed partnership spring up and abide
between the pins and their wearers;
and may that partnership be marked by professional
dedication,
loving-kindness,
and the healing that is yours.

These your daughters and sons, these your hands and feet
give you their trust this morning, Lord.
Pin them with power
as they go out to do what they have promised to do,
As in your name of honor we pray. Amen.

Grand Occasions

Some occasions call for serious, deep, wide, substantive prayers.
When a beloved and important person is moving on to another

position or into retirement, and the setting is foreign to the group (a downtown hotel ballroom, for example), perhaps, or is simply unusually formal, the prayer leader can take the first emotional risk of the evening, searching out and using warm and sincere language. What may be needed is an overview prayer, a "big picture" sharing.

Tribute Dinner Invocation

Almighty God, who dwells beyond and plans,
Patient and caring God, who bends near and listens,
Unspeakably loving God, who abides within and enables,

With stilled spirits, bowed heads, and contrite hearts
We acknowledge your holy presence in this beautiful hall
    made more beautiful by the affirmative purpose that
      has called us here.
We take this one focused moment
    to recognize the mark of your hand in all intersections
      of purpose and opportunity.

You are the master visionary who dreams worlds
    in which people and places
      come together in gracious glory.
So we thank you for the person, [————],
Who was brought together with the place, [————],
    in the city of [————], [*state*],
      where the two became one marvelous,
        amazing, liberating, empowering, joyful,
        firm-stepping, and head-lifted community, and
        sister-brotherhood[15] of intention and design.
[*She or he*] has been our [*woman or man for all seasons*]
    [*our leader of a lifetime*],
And what [*he or she*] has been able to do on campus
    [*in various projects, in various places*],
    in the community,

---

[15]Go ahead! Play with them a little. Have a good time.

among corporate friends,
and in just about every arena
where people gather to hope and aspire
[*Keep returning the honor and the glory to God*]
Has clearly carried your intricacy of motif
and the radiant, gleaming glee you give
to your most favored and treasured acts of creation.

Help us to give and allow [*her or him*] to receive from our
hands, hearts, and voices
the spirit-lifted but tear-sparkled tribute of this evening.
Bless us all as we come;
bless those who have given so generously both tonight
and in these years;
bless those who have planned and labored for this
occasion of celebration;
bless this food, the hands that prepared it and stand
ready to serve;
And bless our [*friend/sister/chief/boss*] because we love
[*her or him*],
and we love what we have been able to do together
while [*she or he*] has been with us.

The victory is [*his or hers*].
The victory is ours.
The victory is yours.

So, in the name that carried us to this day in righteousness
and will, in your mercy,
carry us on from this day in sweet recollection
and newborn determination and appreciation
We pray and say, Amen.

Building Dedication Litany

Just as part of the purpose of congregational singing in worship is to encourage everyone to lift their voices in participation in the experience, prayer litanies involve the assembly in events that they would otherwise simply observe. It is amazing—people who appear casual or even disinterested will, when prompted, join into a prayer litany and appear quite satisfied with the eventual result. There is something special about many voices speaking the same words together and the delicate discovery of the group's speaking rhythm.

Some organizers shy away from litanies at outdoor programs because the unison will be harder to establish. However, the unison does not need to be perfect to be effective. Litanies do require some additional planning and care. The litany needs to be written early and arrangements made for distribution to the assembly. Also, in writing a litany, override your "when in doubt leave it out" training on the use of commas and use them amply. A large number of people reading unfamiliar material aloud together will need all the clues about pausing points they can get. If a tricky phrase or two is unavoidable (see the first *Leader 2* passage below), give them to the leader(s) rather than the group and go over it with them. There is no reason why a litany cannot have more than one leader. Also, the responding group can be divided in interesting ways, as long as the instructions are made clear.

Leader 1:   We mark this occasion because we see that we are changing.

Leader 2:   We mark this occasion because those who came before us taught us to be prayerful in the sight of every change, to be prayerful in the midst of every day.

Assembly: **We mark this occasion because something amazing has happened for us, and the true response must be gratitude.**

Leader 1:   In this new academic center we will come together with important resources at our fingertips.

Leader 2: Our opportunities to learn will be even broader, deeper, and wider than before.

Assembly: And the image we project to the world will be heightened.

Leader 1: This day is about a beautiful building, yet it is more.

[*Next is a reference to the donor of the building.*]

Leader 2: This day is about an intelligent, well-educated, and gracious African American woman, yet it is more.

Assembly: This day is about being blessed in the sight of God and committing ourselves to seek after God's will for this college. "From those to whom much is given, much is expected"; much is expected of us.

Leader 1: So we thank God for [*name, spouse's name*] and for their generosity.

Leader 2: We thank God for having such faith in us that this gift is part of the divine will and plan for this college.

Assembly: We will never forget that in this place and at this time special people stepped forward to support us. Therefore, we commit ourselves to passing the support that we have received on to each other, our school, and our community today and every day. Giving thanks and praise, and giving God the glory, we say— Amen.

Building Dedication Invocation

If a community is really delighted about a project and the project is truly special, there will not be just one event (with prayer), but several. In this instance, there was an event, with prayer, at the groundbreaking, then a topping-off ceremony, then a three-day dedication and celebration with major prayers on two of the three days. The most elaborate prayer was saved for the culminating event.

O Gracious God of the miracle days,
   weaver of wonders and author of opportunities,
With these bowed heads and clasped hands,
   we accept your invitation
   to acknowledge your presence in this auditorium,
      in this building,
         and on this day of celebration and dedication.

Indeed, the things and people we seek to honor here
   were known first to you
      and conceived in the heavenly places.
   [*Next comes an opportunity to "paint the picture" of the building in the prayer.*]

So let every eye that climbs from the luster of marble,
      past the gleam of brass,
   and up toward the glow of polished wood high overhead
      thank you and continue to thank you
   for the blessing of success combined with wisdom,
   creativity given substance through faith, hard work,
      and sacrifice,
         and generosity given life in a special place.

[*As you see, it is possible to celebrate the donors and the building while keeping the focus of the prayer on the great Creator.*]

For this is a living building, a structural being, gifted by you
        with a spirit
Undeniably female—strikingly reflective of the gracious
        and intelligent woman
    after whom she is named,
A nurturing building—loving, encouraging, able, beautiful,
    and capable in her own amazing way
    of giving new life to those who see her,
        new life for faculty and staff who work in her,
        and new life to untold generations of young African
        American women,
Who do now and will continue to perceive themselves and
        their abilities afresh
    in the light of the reality of this academic center.

So we give you glory and praise your holy name,
Thanking you for the givers,
    thanking you and the Drs. Cosby and so many other
        hands and minds
    for the gift—not just a gift of a center,
        but also a gift of trust.

May we strive mightily and prove worthy
        such that praise, knowledge, wisdom,
            strength, humility,
                and lifelong learning[16]
Will not only be the symbols of this celebration
But will also be our hallmark,
    our emblem, our battle cry, and our pledge.

In the name that is above every other name
And keeps our hearts devout,
    even after adoration has left our lips, we pray. Amen.

---

[16]African symbols for thses qualities were the logos for the dedication ceremonies.

Baccalaureate Invocation

O loving and mighty Creator God—

Your gift of this moment comes to us wrapped in robes
    as your [*sons*] [*and*] [*daughters*] are ushered into your
        holy presence
    on this the first of two great days.
We come to stand with them,
    every breathing soul united in spirit and in truth.
Bowed and humble heads adore you.
Folded and submissive hands await you.
    Kum Ba Yah,[17] my Lord.

Receive from us this expression of our most sincere reverence,
    issuing from us in the form of this worship.
Open wide the pathways to heaven
    so that every note and word played, preached, and
    prayed,
        from our souls' clear shouts of glory
        to the quiet murmurings of our hearts,
    might fly straightway to you, there
    and chant a sweet song to you, here.

Dear God, we love you. We praise you.
We exalt you in the time of trouble and in the time of
    triumph.
May your blessing for each of these beloved young [*people*]
    of the Class of [———]
Be as near as your name and as constant as your care.

In the name that is far above any other name
And carries with it our morning joy we pray. Amen.

Another Baccalaureate prayer opening might be:

Now, faith is the substance of things hoped for,
    the evidence of things not seen.[18]

---

[17]Come by here.
[18]Hebrews 11:1 (KJV).

On this day when our hope becomes substance
In the presence of God's faithfulness to us made evident,
Let us join our hearts and minds in prayer.

O loving God of completion and commencement,
    binding tie of our families,
    trustworthy foundation of our friendships,
    enabling power of the fellowship among these
        [*young people*]—

Baccalaureate Litany

Before beginning, the leader explained the "staging" of the litany. The groups that become important after the third stanza were delineated and then were asked to stand before repeating their portion and to remain standing. In this way, by prayer's end all were standing, the graduates having risen last. As a courtesy to wheelchair users and others who may be physically challenged, print "*Those who are able, please stand*" in the program and invite those who do not stand to participate by lifting a hand as they read their portion.

Leader: The fear of the Lord is the beginning of knowledge.

All: **For the Lord gives wisdom. Out of God's mouth come knowledge and understanding.**[19]

Leader: We give thanks this day, O God, for the blessing of this journey made complete in your loving-kindness. We thank you for these young people, poised and ready to take on the new challenges and opportunities you have prepared for them.

Families, Friends, and Guests: We thank you for their lives,
    for their growth, and for their abilities. It is

---

[19]The opening lines are adapted from Proverbs 1:7 and 2:6.

with pride in them and love for you that we call them sons and daughters, brothers and sisters, nieces, nephews, grandchildren, and friends.

Faculty, Staff, Trustees, and Alumni: We praise you for the gift of their presence here at [————]. And for the opportunity to teach and guide them and to share our lives with them, we give thanks.

Graduating Class: We recognize that our education is a gift from God, made real through the efforts of countless people, including ourselves. We will not forget that the hopes of our families, our people, and the needy of this world accompany us as we prepare to leave [————]. With an attitude of gratitude, we proclaim that we are ready to step into our own futures.

Leader: Facing the rising sun of our new day begun,[20] we go forth.

All: O God of goodness and mercy, as you lead, so shall we follow. Amen.

Commencement Invocation

Outside of military ceremonies, there are not too many events that can outdo a college or university commencement ceremony for color, drama, pageantry, and emotion. The people are already "full" before the ceremony begins. The graduates are delighted, the parents are proud, the faculty is satisfied, and the trustees are nostalgic. The prayer leader bringing the invocation can feel free to start "high" and go higher.

---

[20]From "Lift Every Voice and Sing," the Negro national anthem.

This is a good occasion for a prayer that reflects the scene and its impact on the senses. Before preparing, try to find out what sounds will have been heard, what the scene will be like in terms of natural and planned decoration, and how the graduates will be attired. At Spelman I was struck by the look of the young women I was so accustomed to seeing in baseball caps and sneakers elegantly turned out in black mortarboards with blue and white tassels, black robes, and high-heeled black pumps. That prompted this line in a commencement invocation: "Tassel to toe they are living, breathing evidence of your love for us..."

Finally, because commencement ceremonies are long, commencement invocations need to be crisply concise and clear. Keep in mind, also, that in working with outdoor sound systems the speaking pace should be slowed a bit and the diction slightly exaggerated.

From the book of Proverbs, the fourth chapter:
Hear, O [*sons*] [*and*] [*daughters*] of these loving families and
    of God.
  Hear and accept the words of your Creator
    that the years of your lives may be many.
  You are being taught the way of wisdom;
  You are being led in the paths of uprightness.
  When you walk, your step will not be hampered;
    and when you run, you will not stumble.
  Keep hold of instruction, do not let go;
    Guard her, for she is your life.

Let us pray.

For a four-year journey, maybe more,
  full of tests and trials and invitations to strive,
O glorious God of the rising Son,
  maker of heaven and earth and such as we are,
  giver of every good and perfect gift,
We offer you our thanks and praise.

You have made real the dreams
    of these young [*women of African American blood and*
        tradition],
            profound of intellect
            and gorgeous of spirit,
                adorned in cap, cord, and kente[21]
                and crowned with resolve.

Their victory is your might, made visible,
    your mercy, made tangible,
    your mission, given feet and hands.

We pray you will occupy this ceremony
    as your dwelling place
    of celebration and preparation
        and lead us all in your way, everlasting,
As in your name we pray. Amen.

Another way to allow your prayer to capitalize on the look of
commencement might be:

...For through your mercy
    these marvelous young [*people*],
    the pride and hope of a nation,
Are garlanded not only with cord, hood, and kente,
    but also with the glorious colors of your presence;
They are capped not only with mortarboard,
    but also with your strength and your shield;
And your banner over us is love.

---

[21]Kente cloth is the very colorful, hand-woven pride of Ghana. African American students (and others) commonly wear a piece of kente around their necks on very special occasions. At Spelman and other schools, the seniors sometimes have kente specially made in their school colors, with the school name and graduation date woven into the strip.

Commencement Benediction

Class of [*year*]:
 in the vessels of your abilities, your training,
  your background already present,
 and the preparation, persistence, and purpose[22]
  just now beginning to take hold in you,
You carry the hungers and the hopes
 of a people, a nation, and a world.

But there's more.
 As Sweet Honey in the Rock would put it—
  You are your grandmothers' prayers,
  You are your grandfathers' dreamings,
  You are the breath of the ancestors,
  You are the spirit of God.[23]

Follow the path the Lord lights for you,
 and all shall be well.

And now,
 May the Spirit of Truth walk with you each day;
 May the essence of wisdom catch you along the way;
 May the courage of faithfulness hover at your door;
 And may God's steadfast love encircle you forevermore.
  Hallelujah, beloved of the Lord, and Amen.

---

[22]The three points of the Baccalaureate sermon delivered the day before.

[23]Language paraphrased from "We Are." Words and music by Ysaye M. Barnwell © 1993; Barnwell Notes (BMI) from the song suite "Lessons," commissioned by *Redwood Cultural Work's New Spiritual Project,* funded by *Meet the Composer.* Recorded by Sweet Honey in the Rock on *Sacred Ground.*